KAREN MEDLIN

FINDING GOD
IN EVERYDAY PLACES

A Daily Devotional

SILVERSMITH
PRESS

Published by Silversmith Press–Houston, Texas
www.silversmithpress.com

Copyright © 2024 Karen Medlin

All rights reserved.

This book, or parts thereof, may not be reproduced in any form or by any means without written permission from the author, except for brief passages for purposes of reviews. For more information, contact the publisher at office@publishandgo.com.

The views and opinions expressed herein belong to the author and do not necessarily represent those of the publisher.

ISBN 978-1-961093-94-2 (Softcover Book)
ISBN 978-1-961093-95-9 (eBook)

Contents

Week 1		Spending Time with God...................................	1
	Day 1	Son-Light..	3
	Day 2	Such a Wonderful Nutty World............................	6
	Day 3	Jingles...	9
	Day 4	Eye on the Prize	12
	Day 5	Memories..	15
	Day 6	On-Line with God...	18
Week 2		Paid in Full...	21
	Day 1	Pencil Me In	23
	Day 2	The Ruby Necklace	26
	Day 3	Reflections of the Soul...	28
	Day 4	Liquid Joy...	32
	Day 5	The Bunny and The Lamb	35
	Day 6	Clouds of Hope..	38
WEEK 3		Protected under His Wings.................................	41
	Day 1	Birds of a Feather..	43
	Day 2	Wrapped in Arms of Protection.............................	46
	Day 3	Duck, Duck Goose...	49
	Day 4	Hairy Scary Days...	52
	Day 5	Nestle In	55
	Day 6	Help Me!..	59

Week 4		Show and Tell	63
	Day 1	Popping In	65
	Day 2	Too Good Not to Share	68
	Day 3	Game On	71
	Day 4	A Little More Salt, Please	75
	Day 5	Let Love Shine!	78
	Day 6	Wrap Me Up	81
Week 5		Tithe, Rest and Work	83
	Day 1	Determined Life of a Turtle	85
	Day 2	Work Like a Dog	88
	Day 3	Happy Trails	90
	Day 4	Slow Your Roll!	93
	Day 5	God Loves a Good BBQ	96
	Day 6	It All Began with a Leaf	99
Week 6		Praise and Joy	103
	Day 1	Melodies of the Heart	105
	Day 2	Oh, What a Relief!	107
	Day 3	Starry Night	110
	Day 4	Crazy, Beautiful You	113
	Day 5	Color Me Beautiful	116
	Day 6	We're Free to Fly	119
Week 7		Attributes and Attitudes of Christ in Us	123
	Day 1	Breathtaking Peace	125
	Day 2	Wisdom of the Spirit	128
	Day 3	Rockin' It	130
	Day 4	Sweet Memories	133
	Day 5	The Gift of Friendship	136
	Day 6	Strength Training 101	139

Dedication

I am so blessed to have a wonderful group of both family and friends that have encouraged me throughout this journey. I am so thankful to my mom and dad and stepdad for raising me in a Christian home! Looking back over the events of my Christian upbringing, I clearly see how they have shaped my present. I am also thankful to my husband and children, who have given me time, space and encouragement to write this book. And to my sweet circle of friends that I cherish more than you'd ever know ... thank you for allowing me to burden you with questions, having you read yet another entry and sharing with you some of the minute details of the process. Truly, it wouldn't have happened without all of you!

Week 1
SPENDING TIME WITH GOD

God is so worthy of our time. He truly is everywhere! Bible study and prayer time are essential to our spiritual growth. When we spend quality time with our Father, we find our relationship changes. We are taken on the ride of a lifetime with God, Jesus and the Holy Spirit. We start to hear His voice (not necessarily audibly), we see His work in and around our lives and find that even our conversations become richer and deeper. We cultivate this intimate relationship that permeates every aspect of our lives! The way He works is so incredible and indescribable. How can we not take advantage of this unique relationship that was made possible to us through the blood of Christ?

When I personally spend time with the Father, I find that I can spontaneously worship Him all day long. I am now tuned in to where I can see and interact with Him almost everywhere. This is the gift from above!

As we begin this journey, I hope you enjoy finding Him in all the places I do ... and more. I hope this opens your eyes, ears and minds to all the places He is waiting for you to see Him at work in your life!

Week 1, Day 1
SON-LIGHT

But if we walk in the light as He is in the light, we have fellowship with one another, and the blood of Jesus Christ His Son cleanses us from all sin.
1 John 1:7 NKJV

How often do we think to look up and admire the sun above. Of course, we notice when we are driving with that awful, searing glare on the road. But ... do we stop and think about how far away it is and yet is still such a powerful light? Take a moment to close your eyes, throw your head back and feel the sun. Notice the warmth and the light as it shines through your eyelids.

Without the sun, nothing would exist! God did something incredible with this massive ball of fire so far away in the universe. He made the sun to provide us with light and warmth, yet He also created life to interact with the sun. It does so much for us from giving our bodies vitamin D and that deep color in our skin to giving plants the ability to grow and produce food and oxygen for us. Let's not stop

WEEK 1, DAY 1

there ... this far-away star produces heat, seasons, gravity, winds and is a huge player in the water cycle. We haven't even come close to listing all the things the sun gives us, including a sense of joy and wellbeing. Yes, we were created to interact with and draw from the sun ... and from the S-O-N. As powerful as the Sun is, it pales in comparison to Jesus Christ, God's SON.

Yes, we need the sun, but we need Jesus much more. We can bask in His light by reading and meditating on His Word. Just as our physical bodies are tanned and invigorated in the sunshine, our spiritual bodies also radiate our time spent with Jesus. He is our spiritual Son-light. The more time we spend with Him, the more our spirit will become like His if we truly open ourselves to bask in His Word. We need that time spent with God to be able to live in this crazy and unpredictable world of ours. He warms our hearts to others and shines light in our dark places. He brings us peace in hard times and delight in the good times. He will never let go of us because He loves us more than we can ever imagine. He is the gravitational pull to our inner selves where He dwells. We simply cannot get too much of Him.

Can you imagine life without the sun? Can you imagine life without Jesus the Son? That is a life I shiver to imagine. Fortunately, we do not have to face that reality as believers in God the Father, Jesus the Son, and the Holy Spirit! Through Jesus, God has offered us eternal life with Him, and with the Holy Spirit we are never alone! Let us bathe in His Glory!

As essential as the sun to our world, how much more amazing is the gift of His Son! Jesus is an essential part of our Spiritual Life because He is our eternal Life-giver . . .

today, yesterday, and all our tomorrows. His blood covers us with His mighty lifesaving power! The sun, a star that is lightyears away will never even come close to the power and presence of Jesus! Thank You, Father for Jesus the Son!

As we go about our day, may we stop and enjoy the sunshine. Remember the radiance of the Son and thank God for Him. He is the center of our universe. He is the Guiding Light. He is the warmth in our veins ... He is our God Almighty!

Lord God, in the busyness of our day, we pray that we will find time throughout the day to stop and take a second to feel Your presence. Let us recognize the pull inside of us as Your Holy Spirit draws us near to You. May we radiate Your light and warmth to everyone we meet today. Thank You for the sun and, more importantly, thank You for Your Son, Jesus. In His most Holy Name, amen.

Week 1, Day 2
Such a Wonderful Nutty World

And my God shall supply all your needs according to His riches in glory by Christ Jesus.
Philippians 4:19 NKJV

Squirrels are such active and hilariously industrious creatures to watch. Now I know they get a bad rap for finding ways into our attics and such, but ... they are a wonderful part of nature. They quite literally are nature's gardeners. Think of all the nuts and seeds they bury that end up becoming new trees and plants. They have no idea they are gardening when they bury their treats for later. They guard their treasures with a vengeance as I've had one fuss at me for invading his precious territory. It was ok because once I moved on, he didn't hold a grudge. He just went back to his work burying his prized acorns in our yard and yes, a few oak trees did take root.

Squirrels are a great teaching tool for us as Christians. How many seeds has God laid at our feet for us to grab and plant and grow new believers? He provides not only for our physical lives but our spiritual lives as well. Our provisions from God allow us to plant His hope and love everywhere we go. We may not get to see how these seeds germinate and grow, but God will provide others to come along and nurture them. God calls us to share the Good News and His most important command is to Love (Matthew 2:37-39). Wow! God is so good. Planting seeds of love can be the baseline for someone to meet Jesus.

I doubt squirrels give much thought to where their food and their habitats come from; they just do what comes natural to them. How can we plant seeds naturally as we were made to do? Through becoming more and more like Christ. Through prayer, time in the Word and continuous surrendering to the will of God. We need to be in the world, yet not of the world, and a living example of His love. Through our lives, others will see how He cares for us and how much trust we have in Him.

In the above verse, the apostle Paul is writing to the saints in Philippi from—of all places—Prison. You would hardly believe it from the joy in his letter. As he thanks them for their support, he also exhorts them to be humble and united so that they can continue the work of spreading the gospel. What an attitude! He was thankful even in prison ... keeping his eyes fixed on Jesus and spreading that love and joy he had for our Savior! This peace, love, joy and thankfulness allowed Paul to spread the gospel far and wide! His trust was in the Almighty! He wanted his followers and us to continue the work of spreading the gospel as well.

Our attitude and actions allow people to see Christ in our lives and they take notice! How many times have people

WEEK 1, DAY 2

asked for prayers or shared something with you because they know you are a Christian? This is because of the Holy Spirit living within us. His light shines through us as we go through our everyday lives. People see how we rely on God as we make our way through this broken world. We have a Big God that provides for all our needs.

Today, if you happen on a squirrel or a tree—thank God for His glorious provisions. Pray that we will scatter seeds just as joyfully and with as much Love and diligence as that squirrel does! Pray a prayer of thanksgiving for all the "trees" we see that someone long ago planted. I love that everything a Christian life entails is eternal!

Lord God, You are so good to us. We thank You for walking through this life with us and providing everything we need to live a life that brings glory and honor to You. We pray that through our lives, others may come to know You and get to experience the glorious riches only You can provide. In Jesus' Name, amen.

Week 1, Day 3
Jingles

*Tie them as symbols on your hands and
bind them on your foreheads.*
Deuteronomy 6:8

Isn't it interesting how an ad can just stick with us? We go about our day and suddenly find ourselves humming the jingles or spouting their ads as a meme at the appropriate time. In my youth, I loved Mr. Peanut, Mr. Owl and Mr. Bubble and currently we have the "Eat more chicken" and "Where's the beef," not forgetting "I've fallen, and I can't get up." The list goes on and on. Isn't it amazing how some things get imprinted in our minds? Sometimes I can barely recall what I had for breakfast but I am able to recite so many of these catch phrases with ease. Does God's Word seem to be as easily recalled as these cleverly crafted ads that seem to fill up the empty spaces in our minds?

God wants His Word to be just as easily remembered as these catchy ads that grab our attention. Wouldn't it be awesome if His Truth could pop into our mind and out

WEEK 1, DAY 3

of our mouth without much effort? His Word needs to be etched onto our hearts and minds. How can we do this? We must learn scripture and immerse ourselves in His Word. Some verses can be quoted easily like "I can do all things through Christ who strengthens me," or "with God all things are possible." I am sure you have your own personal favorites too.

Deuteronomy 6:5-8 was a command to the Israelites regarding God's Word. He wanted His people to know His commands and to not only follow them but teach them to their children. Some of the Old Testament Jewish rabbis would tie phylacteries on their foreheads and their left arms. These were leather pouches or boxes with scrolls of parchment with scripture written inside them to be a physical reminder of the law of Moses. This not only kept the Word in their hearts and minds but for some, such as the rabbis, it was a physical declaration of their devotion to God.

It is important to God that we know His Word, so we are armed and ready to speak His Truth whenever the opportunity arises. This also makes us more attentive and stronger in the Lord so we can resist the temptation to sin. Doesn't it bring great joy and peace to know His Word is written on our hearts and pressed into our minds where no one can remove it? We can sit and meditate on His Word anytime and anywhere we go. This is a great way to keep our minds on Christ and off the world and its desires. Instead of "I've fallen, and I can't get up," as a Christian our ad might be, "We've fallen, and Christ picks us up!" Praise the Lord!

Today, let the Word of the Lord ring through your thoughts and release that inner joy and thankfulness that He is with you. Let everything we see and do bring to mind

JINGLES

His commands. Whether you are counting how many licks it takes to eat an entire lollipop or hoping for more meat in your sandwich, let His Word come forth from your mind all day long!

Lord God, we are so thankful for Your Holy Word. We pray that it is etched so deeply in our hearts and minds that we can ruminate on it all day long, everywhere we go. Let our joy be rooted in You, and may we always be thankful and mindful of You and ready to speak Your holy scriptures when called to. In Jesus' Name, we pray, amen.

Week 1, Day 4
Eye on the Prize

*So we fix our eyes not on what is seen,
but on what is unseen. For what is seen is temporary
but what is unseen is eternal.*
2 Corinthians 4:18

From baby blues to ebony and all that is in between the eyes are simply captivating. Add a little sunlight and even more color comes bursting forth! Only our amazing Father in heaven could create such an enthralling display of color and depth.

Our eyes display emotion, health, trustworthiness and, of course, vision. We may be able to feign interest in a conversation, but our eyes can give us away! Our pupils will dilate when we are fascinated by someone or something and will constrict when we are tired or bored. I was blown away by that because I thought light and dark was the only thing that caused our pupils to move! Who knew that the eyes could say so much about how we feel! They really are a telling window into our soul!

EYE ON THE PRIZE

Of all the things we find ourselves looking at, there is nothing more important than God. Everything we see, we should look at through His lens. If our eyes are fixed on our Father in heaven, it will change how we see our world around us. This gives us a Kingdom perspective. He looks down at us with love and He truly cares about what we are going through in our everyday lives. I try to remember the Lord is always with me; He sees everything I do, and He hears everything I think and speak. It is so important to take every thought and word spoken, captive to Christ's will.

In 2 Corinthians, Paul has gone through some tough times. However, he keeps his spirit up by keeping his eye on his eternal future with God. Although we cannot see the Spiritual realm, it is all around us. I find comfort in knowing the Lord is with me as I go through the day. I also work to keep my eyes on Him by guarding what I see physically. In the above verse, Paul was exhorting the Corinthians to keep their eyes on what is unseen, that is, the things of the Spirit. There is so much our eyes can take in that will take our focus off of Christ. What our eyes see can feed our thoughts, and before we know it, sin would have crept in. It can come in so subtly you don't even notice when it started. I can hear the children's song by Harry Dixon Loes, "O be careful little eyes what you see"—and it is so true.

One way to guard what our eyes see is through filtering what we watch and read. Not only do I try to censor what I see but I also choose to read from authors that don't use profanity or sexually explicit topics. I also look to nature to bring God and all His glory into focus for me. My eyes take in everything He has created from the sky to the ground. His fingerprints are all around us and focusing on Him is a daily

WEEK 1, DAY 4

goal for me. Just as Paul kept his focus on his eternal future, we should do the same. What great advice for us as well! If we keep our focus off our daily trials and tribulations, and keep it fixed on kingdom thoughts instead of worldly thoughts, we can then look to the prize which is heaven!

As you go about your day, strive to keep your eyes on the unseen. Guard what your eyes see, pray to the Lord continuously and stay in His Word. Suddenly we will find our thoughts naturally landing on the Lord. And that is a very good place to be!

Lord, how incredible is this body You created! The eyes are such a beautiful part of us and are unique to each of us! I pray we use our eyes to focus on You and to guard them from things that can cause us to stumble. In Jesus' Name, amen.

Week 1, Day 5
Memories

*I remember the days of long ago; I meditate on all
your works and consider what your hands have done.*
Psalm 143:5

It's hard not to smile as we leaf through old pictures and take a walk back through time. Usually, it's happy moments we've captured among those we love and cherish. I can lose myself in memories as I get transported back in time with these precious pieces of my life. It's even easier to capture events of our lives today with our phone camera continuously on our person. Before 1825 this wasn't even possible. Once, only professionals had the capability to take a picture and in the biblical days, it was only by means of drawings and the written or spoken word. Even twenty years ago, memories were captured a lot differently. It is easy to forget how blessed we are to be able to freeze moments in time with such ease.

In our passage today, the psalmist is remembering all that God had done in and around him and is meditating

WEEK 1, DAY 5

on his memories. The word "remember" according to the Christian bible reference is used in the KJV 148 times in the bible. Wouldn't it be grand to have pictures of each time the Lord worked in our lives? Jesus wants us to remember Him in all we do. He is our very reason for life! I would love to have had pictures of Jesus growing up—as a baby, little boy and up through adulthood. Instead, we are instructed to know Him through His Word so that when He returns we will recognize Him. I believe this to be a blessing . . . we will know Him intimately in our heart and not by sight. If we truly know Him, no imposter will be able to trick us and claim to be the Christ! (Matthew 24:5). But this also means we need to really study His word so that we do recognize Him.

In my bible, I once decided to start at the beginning and read all the highlighted and underlined scriptures. Every passage that spoke to me I left a mark. Over the years since I received that bible as a high school graduation gift from my church in 1987, I have read those passages again and again. Some came with memories of places I was at when I marked the page. If you have never done this, I highly recommend taking a stroll through memory lane with your bible. I love reading all the passages that stood out for me throughout my Christian journey. What sweet memories of the times I have spent in His Word! I can also go back and read just what is in red—Jesus' words. I am so blessed by this exercise! I Love His Word!

Our bibles are such intimate representations of what we have learned from God. I cherish my grandfather's bible that I inherited after he died. It is one of the most treasured items I own. I love the faded pencil marks and notes he

MEMORIES

wrote in the margins. I imagine when I pass on from this life, my bible will lie in the hands of my family. Every mark and highlighted passage will be read by someone else long after I am gone. Look through your bible and meditate on what the Lord has done in your life. Remember the times His Word has upheld you, comforted you, encouraged you, and taught you. The Lord has allowed this book to survive through generations and we should cherish His Words in our hearts.

Today, thank the Lord for the Bible and spend time perusing its pages. Just as we have photos of our lives, we have the Bible to be the spiritual photo album that records our faith walk. Let the sweet memories bring you great joy as you meditate on all that He has done for you. I would like to pray Hebrews 4:12 including the blurb below that the elders of my church wrote to me as I entered my adult life:

Lord God, Your Word is living and active and sharper than any two-edged sword, piercing as far as the division of soul and spirit, of both joints and marrow, and able to judge the thoughts and intentions of the heart. Thank You for Your Word and may we Know Christ the Lord intimately through the study of the scriptures, the greatest book in the world! Lord, this book truly has the most noble ideas and the most sacred thoughts. These words come from the mind of God, written by the hand of man, for the salvation of the world. May we use it wisely, read it often and trust in it always! In Jesus' Name, amen.

Week 1, Day 6
On-Line with God

The mind governed by the flesh is death, but the mind governed by the Spirit is life and peace ...
Romans 8:6

I cannot count how many ways I can fall into the proverbial rabbit hole. Social media, funny videos, binge watching tv ... the list goes on. All of us can get consumed with these time fillers. We innocently go in to check email, then hit a link and end up somewhere in cyberspace. One minute seems to instantly become hours. Sometimes it's bedtime and I'm just not tired enough to fall asleep. I turn on the tv only planning to watch one episode and suddenly I've wasted my precious time of rest for the empty hours of television. Let's not even go into the social media realm where time does not exist!

The all-consuming price of getting stuck in these activities is time lost that we will never get back. Perhaps I'll face a sleepy day after staying up too late or I won't get all the necessary chores done. Even playing games can become not only time consuming but addictive as well. No matter what has pulled me in, I am filled with an anxious, empty feeling of the time I wasted away. On the other hand, time spent with the Lord is never wasted. We don't leave that time with Him empty and at sea. According to Statista in 2024 the average social media usage time was 143 minutes per day. So, I ask, how many minutes are we spending daily on bible study? Ouch, this is a sobering thought on where our priorities are set.

In Romans we are told by Paul that if our minds are set on spiritual things, our desires will be tuned into what the Holy Spirit desires. We spend time with Him and know Him and when we go forth and act on what we have read, that is pleasing to the Lord. When we are consumed with the Lord, we feel sated, refreshed, encouraged and alive. God loves us so much! He needs to be with us all the time, the landing place to where we find our thoughts drifting.

Typically, our hearts are where our thoughts are and, sadly, many times they are not on Him. The internet has made it too easy for us to drift off into cyber space. Of course, we can find good sermons and devotionals online but we need to beware of the pitfalls of being distracted by other links at our fingertips. We do not want to neglect God and get caught up in the desires of this world. We want Him right here with us in our hearts. Let Him consume us and be our every breath. He will never leave us feeling as if we have wasted time. He will not only renew us with His love and compassion but allow us to share our knowledge of Him with those around us. We have logged in to His blessed life!

Today, when you find yourself logging into your favorite website, take a detour to an online bible and spend that

WEEK 1, DAY 6

time with God or a bible trivia game. When you reach for a book, let it be the bible, bible study or even a Christian fiction book. When you choose a radio station, let it be praise music. We have so many different opportunities to worship and praise our Father in Heaven. Let us meditate on what is good, noble, just, pure, lovely, good report and praiseworthy as we are commanded in Philippians 4:8. Now that is time well spent!

Lord God, we have so much at our fingertips. Distractions appear as soon as we open our eyes in the morning. Father, sometimes we feel as if life is going at warp speed, and it is so easy to get lost in our own world. Lord, draw us to You and give us the desire to spend the first fruits of our time with You. In Jesus' Name, I pray, amen.

Week 2
PAID IN FULL

Jesus is the reason for our Hope! Because of His saving grace, we are able to come before God with confidence our sins have been forgiven and we are heaven-bound. I am so thankful for this because dealing with my human weaknesses is often frustrating! Much as I hate sin, I struggle with it at times. There is so much to be thankful for; but the number one priority is Jesus who died for my sinfulness! He who knew no sin became sin for me so that I could become the righteousness of God (2 Corinthians 5:21).

The price for our sin has been PAID IN FULL! He is our treasure, He is our light, and His Love is our firm foundation. I pray you will be blessed this week as you continue to find Him in your everyday life. May the bounty of His love spill over into every corner of your world!

Week 2, Day 1
Pencil Me In

For we are God's workmanship, created in Christ
Jesus to do good works, which God prepared
in advance for us.
Ephesians 2:10

When I was in elementary school, I loved to pull out a brand-new pencil. It was perfect and shiny, and the eraser stood tall on the end like a perfect little top hat. I would head over to the sharpener to make a perfect pointed tip and would head back to my desk to write. Well, we all know the story. The tip was so pointy that as soon as I applied the pressure to write, it would break off, graphite marking the page and then that perfect eraser top had to be used to erase the graphite blob that is now marring my page. Now, I could have just pulled out the old pencil with the used eraser and kept the new one in the pencil box so it wouldn't get messed up; but then I wouldn't have that moment of pure joy when I could bring out the new one.

It makes me smile even to remember that feeling when

WEEK 2, DAY 1

the tip broke off! Sigh ... if only that were my biggest issue of the day, huh? I'm certain back in the day when pencils were nothing more than a piece of graphite wrapped in string, the same elation would happen when they received the new piece with the fresh string! Oh, how we love to have new and fresh things to use in our everyday lives!

God sent us Jesus so that we can be clean and fresh and new! His blood washes us clean so that we can rise anew every day. When we pray, repent and turn from our sinful ways, isn't it wonderful to know we are as shiny and new spiritually as that brand new pencil? The above scripture shows that He is proud of us because we are His "workmanship." The Greek word for "workmanship" is *poiema*, which reminds me of "poem." We are indeed His poem, and He delights in us.

God created us to do good works and, yes, we may get marred from time to time. But if we don't get out there and do His Will, then we will be no more useful than that shiny pencil left in the box. It would be impossible to foresee all that we will write with this pencil and what impact those written marks may serve. Even loaning that pencil out to someone might make their day! Every groove and chip and even shrinkage from use never takes away its purpose. The best part is Christ is our eraser! When we make a mistake, we confess it to Him, and He erases it like it never happened.

Today, as we go through our day let us remember to let the Lord use us for His divine purpose and not be stowed away in a drawer somewhere. Let us get out there and experience the joy He has set out for us and let us not grow weary of our journey. May we leave marks of Christ everywhere we go! And don't forget to pencil in some time with the Lord as well!

PENCIL ME IN

Lord God, we come before You with thankful hearts. You sent Your Son Jesus to save us from our sinful selves. We are so grateful that His perfection and sacrifice are open to all who call upon the name of Jesus. Because of this, we can come before You shiny and new, with a humble and repentant heart, full of love and devotion to You. Lord, continue to grow us and stretch us so we may leave marks of Your love everywhere we go. In Jesus' Name, amen.

Week 2, Day 2
The Ruby Necklace

But store up for yourselves treasures in heaven, where moth and rust do not destroy, and where thieves do not break in and steal.
Matthew 6:20

I am not a huge jewelry wearer; however, there are some things I have been given that mean a lot to me. I'm very sentimental and can easily tell people exactly who gave me whatever tchotchke or jewelry or whatever. One such item I have is a small ruby pendant necklace that belonged to my grandmother. I inherited this sweet gem as a gift from my aunt. It is not worth much money but it's not the earthly value that makes me treasure it; it's the sentimental value attached to it. It was given to me in love, and this tiny, old ruby necklace is worth more to me than any expensive ruby necklace. If it were ever lost or stolen, I would be heartbroken.

Sometimes tangible things are a treasure to us because they make us feel a connection to family, friends or even a sweet moment in time. God wants us to feel that kind of connection with Him. Our greatest treasure should be Jesus. There is nothing on this earth that can compare to Him. Nothing. Nothing. Only Jesus can love us, save us and fill us to the brim with our heavenly hope. He is a gift with no price tag because He laid down His life for us freely. If we stay true to Him, no one can steal Him away from us and nothing on earth can destroy His presence. We are indeed the recipients of the most expensive treasure on this earth!

Sit for a moment and let this marinate in your mind ... Jesus Is Our Treasure. Is there anything on this earth more valuable to you than Christ? Is there anything else in this world that you can take with you everywhere you go? Is there anything you own that cannot be stolen or broken? Only Jesus Christ fits the bill. He paid the price. He is our treasure. He is the pearl of great price that a merchant who discovered it sold everything to buy (Matthew 13:45-46).

As much as I treasure my grandmother's ruby necklace, I would gladly give it up for Christ. He loved me so much that I have the confidence in my salvation to know that I will be reunited with Him in heaven along with all the other believers in Christ. That knowledge is so overwhelming to me and fills me with so much love and gratitude.

Today, focus your mind on knowing you are part of the heavenly kingdom of God because of Jesus! Look at the things you treasure and know they cannot measure up to the riches found in Christ Jesus.

Lord God, we pray our true treasure will always be found in Jesus. He is worth more than anything this world has to offer. You are the everlasting God who loved us so much You sent Your Son to sacrifice everything for us. Thank You, Lord, God! In Jesus' Name, amen.

Week 2, Day 3
Reflections of the Soul

> *Anyone who listens to the word but does not do what it says is like a man who looks at his face in a mirror and after looking at himself, goes away and immediately forgets what he looks like.*
> James 1:23-24

I love mirrors! They can make a room look bigger, reflect other images, function as safety devices on our cars and, of course, are essential when we are getting dressed. Over time, mirrors have improved greatly from when they were made using stone and volcanic glass and metals like copper and bronze. Our modern-day mirror, usually made of aluminum and glass, gives us a much clearer image.

What image do you see when you look into the mirror? Imagine staring at yourself, walking away, and being unable to recall what you look like. Or worse, looking into your reflection and not recognizing the person looking back at you. What about your spiritual mirror. Do you see what God has commanded you to be in your spiritual life? Do you see actions and thoughts that reflect what you have been taught by Christ? What comes to mind? Or do you see yourself through the blood of Christ?

James used the analogy of the mirror to make a point. Jesus fulfilled all the requirements of the law of Moses and freed us from the consequence of breaking the law—which is sin and death (Romans 3:23). We are no longer bound by sin, guilt and shame, and by grace we can live according to His law, the law of Christ (Galatians 6:2) His is the perfect law that gives freedom!

By James' day, the Jewish people had many laws that went beyond the Torah, known as the law of Moses. Over time, the intent of these laws became blurred just as the mirrors of old showed blurred images. The laws became less about God and more about the minute religious rituals and observances imposed on them by their religious leaders. For example, the command to keep the Sabbath holy was meant to make the Sabbath a day of rest, set apart for God. However, the religious leaders went on to interpret "work" as anything requiring the slightest effort such as cooking or washing dishes.

You see, the original intent of the law in the Old Testament was not to make people law-abiding robots, but to be guidelines to teach the people righteousness and relationship with God. They were a shadow of the new law of Christ which is based on the principles He taught in His Sermon on the Mount in (Matthew 5). These can be summed up in two commands: *"'Love the Lord your God with all your heart and with all your soul and with all your mind.' This is the first and greatest commandment. And the second is like it: 'Love your neighbor as yourself'"* (Matthew 22:37-39).

WEEK 2, DAY 3

Jesus' death and resurrection meant that the old laws had passed but the spiritual principles behind those laws still stand: *"Thou shall have no other gods before Me, remember the sabbath day to keep it holy, thou shalt not kill, thou shalt not commit adultery, thou shalt not steal,"* and so on (Exodus 20:1-17 KJV). No longer are we burdened by the old laws established in the Old Testament but now to live holy lives through grace. Jesus, like our current mirror is a clear reflection of what our lives should look like as new Covenant believers.

If we find ourselves living a life of condemnation, not following the ways of Christ, not bearing fruit for the kingdom, perhaps we need to take a good hard look in the mirror. Let's examine ourselves to see what needs to change in our lives to be able to reflect Christ daily. James' message to the people of old still stands true today. If we have studied the Word and then go about our lives not reflecting Christ, it is equivalent to looking into a mirror and then forgetting what you look like.

Today, examine yourself in the Spiritual mirror and define what you see. If you are not living in the blessed freedom of Christ, it's time to make a change. If you see yourself growing consistently closer to the image of Christ, thank Him and stay in the Word, and in prayer and fellowship with other believers. Praise be to God that He sent his Son to die so that we no longer have to live a life of legalism and condemnation!

Lord God, thank You so much for the freedom granted through Christ Jesus. We are so thankful He broke the chains that bound us to the old laws. We are now free to come before You, confess our sins and live a life of grace and truth. As we look into the mirror of our souls, please show us any places within our hearts that need to be adjusted so that Christ can radiate within and through us. In Jesus' Name, amen.

Week 2, Day 4
Liquid Joy

*But Jesus answered, "I tell you the truth.
Unless you are born from water and the Spirit,
you cannot enter God's kingdom."*
John 3:5 ICB

What a precious gift of God is water! We are so blessed to have fresh, running water. We have so much water, we can collect it in a cement basin and swim in it, and water our lawns until it spills onto the streets and sidewalks. For most of us, if we find ourselves needing water, it's usually as easy as walking to the kitchen or if out and about, heading to the nearest convenience store.

But out of all the uses of water the most important is its use by God as a symbol of salvation through baptism. We are saved by our faith, but the water is the symbol of our baptism into His death!

I still remember the evening I was baptized into Christ. A good friend phoned one Sunday afternoon, and we talked about baptism. We were eleven at this time, but we began our faith journey in bible class and church from a very young age. As each of us matured in our faith, we found our heart for Jesus Christ as our savior. That Sunday evening, we each declared our pledge of faith and in obedience to Christ, were baptized. What an incredible evening to share with such a good friend.

I remember pronouncing my faith and being dipped under the water. As I was lifted, I remember feeling so joyful, refreshed, and ready to take on my faith walk. The warm, baptismal water that night felt different from all other waters I had ever experienced. That was the water where I made my first act of obedience to Christ. I was saved by my faith and then acted through obedience as I was submerged into the water that represented my purification. I had died to my sinful nature and risen in newness of life (Romans 6:4). That was my life-giving water!

Nothing compared to that evening in the warm baptismal water of our church. The Spirit of the Lord filled me that evening! Obviously that warm water isn't what saved me. It was my acceptance into Christ by my public declaration of faith and following His call to be washed clean by the waters that represented His blood on the cross. This was the night I declared my intent to follow Jesus until I fully entered the Kingdom of Heaven!

In our scripture Jesus commands us to be born of water AND Spirit for salvation. Praise the Lord He bore our sins on the cross. His blood symbolically washed me clean before God and man that night! I am saved and set free all because of that brutal sacrifice of an innocent man, a man that could have saved Himself but instead chose death so that all those before and after Him could be right with God. Hallelujah!

WEEK 2, DAY 4

Today, let the water we use throughout the day be a reminder of our commitment to Christ Jesus. Let our heart, speech and walk all be aligned with the will of our Father in heaven as He continuously washes our sins away. He sent His Son to be the ultimate sacrifice for our sins. He alone is mighty to save, and we are forever grateful for that sacrifice!

Lord God, we come before You with thankful hearts for sending Your Son to this earth. He lived life fully human and yet fully and divinely part of the Holy Trinity. He allowed Himself to be tortured, shamed and killed on the cross as the ultimate sacrifice for our sinfulness. We gratefully accept this gift of salvation and pray we live our lives as dedicated followers of Christ Jesus. In His Holy Name we pray, amen.

Week 2, Day 5

The Bunny and The Lamb

"For I tell you, I will not eat it again until it finds fulfillment in the kingdom of God."
Luke 22:16

The rabbit is one of my favorite animals. When spring approaches I know the Easter season will be coming upon us and everywhere I look is an Easter Bunny. Funny that our current day Easter mascot is the bunny. The Easter egg can be traced back in time to Russia. The Russians used to make these ornate eggs and give them as gifts. Over time, this tradition spread into Germany, and it was the German immigrants that brought this tradition to us in America.

The meaning of Easter today looks quite a bit different from Christ's day. The original celebration during our current time of Lent and Easter was the Passover with the Israelites. Every year they would commemorate their exodus from Egyptian slavery by the hand of God. This was when God instructed the Israelites to slaughter a lamb, eat it, and place the blood of the lamb over the door. This is how

WEEK 2, DAY 5

the angel of death knew to pass by that door so that the entire household was spared (Exodus 12:1-13). In the New Testament the Passover Lamb was Jesus.

As soon as Jesus came into public ministry, John the Baptist declared Him to be the Lamb of God (John 1:29). When the third Passover feast came upon them before Jesus' crucifixion, He instructed His disciples to make all the preparations for this feast. Unbeknownst to them, they were setting up Jesus' last Passover here on earth. He stated that He would not be partaking of this again until He returned. He told His disciples during this important meal to remember Him through the bread as His body, and the cup as His blood. The disciples had no idea what would lie ahead for Jesus. Jesus was telling them to remember Him when they ate this meal (Matthew 26:17-30).

No longer would they be looking back to the Exodus from Egypt but forward to the Exodus from sin and the clutches of the devil. The blood that was painted above their doorframes to save them from the angel of death would now be spilled on the cross. Christ was the final sacrifice since He took on the sins of man and gave up His perfect, sin-free life as the ultimate sacrifice. Every time we eat the bread and drink the wine, we are commanded to remember His sacrifice on the cross. We can now look forward to sharing this meal with Him when He returns.

When the Easter season is upon us, let it be a time of remembrance of all God has done for us through His Son Jesus Christ. As a kid, Easter was about the bunny, the eggs, the candy, and the clothes. As we mature, we learn that it's not about the bunny, but about the Lamb. The Lamb that sacrificially let Himself be slain by man. The Lamb that was separated from God for three days. The Lamb that overcame death by rising to life after three days. This is Easter! Many Christians called it "Resurrection Sunday."

Today, let us keep Christ in the forefront of our thoughts when the Easter season begins. When we see all the commercials for candy and eggs, let us be reminded of the Lamb. Jesus is everything we need yesterday, today, and tomorrow. Praise the Lord for His sacrifice and for His resurrection! Let's hop to it and spread the Word that He is risen!!!

Lord God, no words can describe our thankfulness for Jesus and His sacrifice. There is nothing on this earth that can equate with the Love He has for us, and we have nothing but our devotion and worship to give back to You. Thank You for loving us so much that You sent Jesus to redeem us from our sins. In Jesus' Name, we pray, amen.

Week 2, Day 6
Clouds of Hope

After that, we who are still alive and are left will be caught up with them in the clouds to meet the Lord in the air. And so we will be with the Lord forever.
1 Thessalonians 4:17

Who doesn't love those puffy, fluffy, airy clouds that dot the sky with thousands of pictures. When I was a little girl, I always imagined it was where the angels lived. I wanted to go up and lie down in the clouds with the angels! When I was seven years old, I boarded an aircraft and sadly discovered the clouds were not the magical home of the angels but a smoky mist that obstructed my view. I later learned in school that the clouds are part of the water cycle. Well, even if they are nothing more than visible water droplets in the sky, I still find them a magical, peaceful place. And one day, other believers and I will get whisked up to those wonderful, puffy, fluffy clouds where we will meet Jesus.

Today's verse in 1 Thessalonians speaks about the day believers who are still alive on this earth will get to meet

CLOUDS OF HOPE

up in the clouds with Christ and the ones who have already died. Wow! What a vision! Oh, this gives me chill bumps! This verse takes me back to that magical vision I had of the clouds as a child. All of us will be together with Christ in the clouds awaiting our transport into heaven. I can't wait to see so many who have gone on before me and I know you have a list of people as well. Nothing I can envision will even come close to the actual event. I love to ponder what that day might look like. My mind cannot fathom all the glorious beauty that awaits those that are saved, and heaven bound.

Clouds are often mentioned throughout the Bible in relation to God's love for His creation. In both the Old and New Testament, we find clouds mentioned but the New Testament is where we will land today. The ascension scene in Acts 1:9-11 gives us a pretty clear idea of how Jesus left and how we can expect Him to return. Take a moment to look this passage up and meditate on it for a bit. John writes of Christ, *"Look, He's coming with the clouds, and every eye will see Him, even those whom pierced Him and all the peoples of the earth will mourn because of Him"* (Revelation 1:7).

I think the description given by Paul and John fits together seamlessly with Thessalonians 4:17. Those left on the earth will be looking up into the sky in wonder and terror as those of us who love the Lord are united with Him in the clouds. As a Christ-following believer, that vision brings me such peace, joy and hope! If you or someone you love is not part of this family of believers, I encourage you to share this joyful expectation with them! Let them see what a wonderful day of reunion we will be encountering! He wants no one to miss out!

Today, when you look up into the sky and ponder those

WEEK 2, DAY 6

clouds of hope, can you envision Jesus appearing suddenly and floating down? Let the clouds be a reminder to meditate on Jesus' mercy and love, for His guiding hand in our lives, and the hope we have in Him as we await His return. Oh, how my soul thirsts for Him! Lord, bring on those Clouds of Hope!

Lord God, the full glory of You cannot be fathomed by us but we want to stop, worship and praise Your Holy Name. Let the clouds be a continuous reminder of the hope we have in Jesus' return. Although the time and place is not known, we are so thankful for Your guiding hand in our lives and the promise of His return we find in Your Holy Scriptures. In Jesus' Most Powerful and Glorious Name, amen.

Week 3
PROTECTED UNDER HIS WINGS

On this earth troubles come and go like the wind. Sometimes trouble seems to want to come and sit for a spell. Fortunately, we have a refuge called Jesus. The best medicine for an anxious heart is focusing our eyes and minds on the Eternal. Somehow, a peace that you just cannot explain wraps itself around your soul like a warm breeze on a cool day. You can't explain it but you sure do feel it! When we find ourselves on the other side of it, we look back and see He was right there with us all along!

    No matter the season you find yourself in today, I pray this week you might join me in His precious Word. May He fill every anxious nook and cranny inside of us! No one knows us like our Creator! Praise God!

Week 3, Day 1
Birds of a Feather...

*Though one may be overpowered,
two can defend themselves. A cord of
three strands is not quickly broken.*
Ecclesiastes 4:12

Birds of a feather flock together is an old English saying that refers to how like species of birds gather together. They do this for protection from predators. This brings to mind a hawk trying to roost in one of our backyard trees and these two blue jays that were having none of it. In fact, those two small birds ran that big raptor off! Not sure if one would've been as successful.

    Flocking together with Christian friends can serve the same purpose. Yes, we have fun but here is where we find love, encouragement, and protection. It is so much easier to tackle a difficult situation with back up! Although God is always with us, He knows we do best when we have others to walk this road of life along with us. Our Christian brothers and sisters are where we can circle the wagons! This is

WEEK 3, DAY 1

our safe haven! God is with us, and He has provided this small army to not only do battle, but to celebrate life with us. Isn't it wonderful to know someone is praying with and for you to the Lord?

At the same time, I've come across people at church who never found their niche. My first question is always, "Have you been involved in a life group or bible study? If not, then come on and let's get to it!" It's important to realize that, yes, sometimes God drops someone into our life that just fits. Most of the time though we have to put ourselves out there. If you asked any of my group of close friends where we met, it would be through teaching or attending a class together or participating in some kind of activity. It is hard to connect one on one with others in a large setting, so we need to seek out opportunities to meet and interact with others. Just as we actively pursue a mate or a job, we also must actively pursue friendships—and this includes at church.

Fortunately, we know we already have something in common: our faith! Having these connections over time will deepen and, before you know it, you are doing life with God alongside other friends. This is so important because we need the support of our brothers and sisters in Christ to fight the devil and the desires of this world! And believe me ... I do get called out from time to time because they love me.

We can find divine protection through God no matter where we might be. However, we are less likely to succumb to the devil's schemes when we purposely draw near to God in fellowship with other believers. If we consistently spend time in His word as well as stay in communion with our Christian family, we become stronger in the Lord. I have found that I always feel comforted and encouraged after hanging out with

BIRDS OF A FEATHER...

my Christian friends. To have this bond takes effort. We must make a conscious effort to spend time with one another. If we let our busyness get in the way, we play right into Satan's hand. If he can divide us, it leaves us more vulnerable to attack. Hebrews 10:25 exhorts us not to neglect meeting together. 1 Peter 5:8 is another verse that reminds us Satan is lurking and seeking someone to devour just like a lion on the hunt. Staying in communion with others strengthens and supports us. God knew we needed each other.

While there are many verses in the bible about Christian bonds, this verse in Ecclesiastes especially reminds us how we need to bond ourselves to those He blesses us with. When we gather with our brothers and sisters in Christ it is pleasing to the Lord, and He says He is there with us. When we are together and able to exhort, comfort and encourage each other, we leave refreshed, stronger, and more ready to take on the world. This is an intimate relationship that today's verse is talking about. We get to draw on this strength to stand firm in our beliefs, and hopefully draw others among our Christian brother- and sister-hood into a relationship with Jesus.

Wherever you find yourself today, let the birds be a reminder of how God has placed in your path your flock of friends. Take time to pray to the Lord with thanksgiving for the network of friends He has provided you for your protection and for His never-ending goodness.

Lord, thank You for the Christian friends You have provided in our lives. May we encourage and strengthen each other in the name of the Father! Protect us and let the glue that holds us together be rooted in love and devotion for You. In Jesus' Name, amen.

Week 3, Day 2
Wrapped in Arms of Protection

The Lord is good, a refuge in times of trouble.
He cares for those who trust in Him.
Nahum 1:7

As I went to feed my husband's fish, I sat and watched them swim around their saltwater habitat. I took in all their interactions—where they liked to hide and where they liked to swim.

The most interesting of them all were these two clown fish that seemed to dance in between the tentacles of this sea anemone. None of the other fish even came close to the beautiful anemone. This sparked my interest, so I researched and learned that the clown fish and the sea anemone have a symbiotic relationship. This is a win-win relationship. The clown fish feed on some tasty morsels they find in the anemone. The anemone, in turn, get a nice cleansing from the clown fish as well as some tasty food. The clown fish are able to hide in these poisonous stinging tentacles because they have a protective film on their bodies not found on other fish. This creates a nice little relationship between these two sea creatures and quite a bonus for the clown fish—safe refuge!

The same way the clown fish find protection in the arms of the anemone, we too find protection in the arms of Christ. Just as the clown fish have a film that protects them from being stung, we are enveloped by the presence of the Lord. As I look in on their world, I imagine how God looks in at us. I can see all around the fish tank, above, below and inside. I can see if the water is low, if they need to be fed, if the temperature is correct or if the tank needs to be cleaned. I can see if any of them is sick and needs to be cared for, and I can watch their behavior to see if they are happy and healthy. They know me as their provider, and when I come near, they quickly swim out to see me.

When the Lord comes near, do we recognize Him? Do we come out to get fed? Do we cling to Him and know He is our refuge? He sees everything and knows everything about us, and He loves us. Just as the clown fish stay near to the anemone for protection and care, we also should stay near to the Lord for His protection and care. It is so amazing how many examples there are in nature of the Love and care of God. He has provided everything each species here on earth needs to survive. He has provided us everything we need to get through life. He tells us not to worry, that He is good, and He will protect those who are willing to trust Him.

Today, remember who our protector is, and thank God for His provisions for us. Let us remember that He knows what is best for us. We might not see danger around the corner, but He does. He is a perfect Father! What a wonderful example nature gives us in this sweet underwater

WEEK 3, DAY 2

friendship of trust and provision! As He does for even the most insignificant of His creation, how much more will our Lord and Savior do for us! How blessed are we to have such a loving Father! Can we trust in Him? I hope the answer from each and every one of us is yes!

Lord God, as You look down on Your creation and those that follow You, we ask that You protect us and draw us near to You. Let us not stray away and get stung by the evils of the world. Let us always rest inside Your loving arms and trust You to protect us and fight our battles. In Jesus' Name, amen.

Week 3, Day 3
Duck, Duck Goose

The Lord is with you, He is mighty to save. He will take great delight in you, He will quiet you with His love, He will rejoice over you with singing.
Zechariah 3:17

There is a lake in my neighborhood that I love to walk around. It is always a hotbed of activity, mostly turtles and ducks, but we see fish jump, dragonflies dance on the water, snakes sunning, geese relaxing and cranes standing like kings over the lake watching for their next meal. My favorite are the downy, baby ducks and there are usually around twelve following mama and daddy around, but sadly they rarely all survive with all the predators around. The chicks rely very heavily on mama to protect and nurture them. If mama duck sees anyone getting too close, she will begin her rhythmic quacking and all her chicks quickly fall into line and follow her wherever she leads them.

Like those baby ducks, do we recognize our Father's voice when He sees danger getting too close to us? Mama

WEEK 3, DAY 3

duck has her brood to raise and keep up with, but God has millions of children, and He can perfectly watch over each and every one of us. He knows our every thought and need. He created us in His own image, and He cares deeply for each one of us. He knows exactly what is going on with us and where we are headed. Nothing escapes His attention. He lovingly calls us away from danger and comforts us in our times of need. Like momma duck, He will cover us with His feathers, and provide refuge under His wings (Psalm 91:4).

Although our Lord calls us to Him, when He sees us getting too close to something that can hurt us, He also gives us free will. Think if that little duckling doesn't heed his momma's call, what fate may await him. A hungry snake or a dispirited goose could end the life of one of these little ones. As for us, we have the Holy Spirit within us to help guide us; but the key for us is recognizing the nudges, and then following His call. Sometimes we need to really stop the busyness that tends to engulf us and just wait on the Lord's direction. Sometimes we don't heed the call, and end up heading down the wrong road. If we continue down the wrong path, it will lead to destruction, spiritual death is not something to take lightly.

Walking the road to eternal life is not always an easy path to follow. But when we walk with the Lord, isn't it a comfort to know that if we stray, He will come to call us back just as the mama duck calls her chicks? He will quiet us with His love when our lives get hard, and He takes great delight over us with every happy and victorious moment we encounter. The Lord rejoices over us, and it brings Him great pleasure to see us follow His will and bring others to Christ.

DUCK, DUCK GOOSE

Today, let this verse be infused into our souls. Let us be totally present to see how our Lord walks with us, and listen for His gentle, guiding voice. Take captive every thought and take every opportunity to thank the Lord for all He does for us. Just like the ducklings, let us follow Jesus all the time. There is nothing quite like the victorious life in Christ with Him leading us on!

Lord God, help us to take note of Your nudges and hear Your voice when danger lurks. Help us to be fully present with You and to know Your voice so intimately that we can heed Your call, and follow where You lead us. Protect us, Lord, from the dangers that surround us. May we be blessed beyond comprehension by following You everywhere You lead us. In Jesus' Name, amen.

Week 3, Day 4
Hairy Scary Days

"Indeed, the very hairs of your head are all numbered. Don't be afraid; you are worth more than many sparrows."
Luke 12:7

My little towheaded baby boy was born bald as a cue ball. Thankfully, it didn't take long for that downy soft, light blond hair to come in and I couldn't keep my hands off it! That beautiful, fine, white, silky hair finally did darken some with age, but the memory of that sweet baby hair always makes me smile. At the time I had never heard the term towheaded and thought people were telling me my beautiful little angel had a head that looked like a big toe. Finally, I found out that it meant the color of his hair was like the color of flax. And His Father in heaven knew each and every battle he would fight, each and every success along the way and, of course, when each and every hair would emerge from his precious, bald head.

Isn't it wonderful that our Father knows us so intimately?

HAIRY SCARY DAYS

When these words were uttered by Jesus in Luke 12, He was talking with His disciples. Jesus was letting them know how precious they were to the Father and they need not be afraid. We too can cast all our fears, concerns, and cares on our Lord. He knows where we are and what we face. Just as a child looks to his parents for protection, we can look to God. And, the disciples could look to God as well. After all, they were in the very presence of God in human form ... Jesus!

The disciples were fearful of what the Pharisees would do to those who followed Christ. This was a very real fear and for good reason. Many Christ followers were persecuted, but Christ wanted them to be able to confidently face those who terrorized them. Yes, they could be persecuted, but only in this life. God is the all-powerful one who is to be feared by those who do not know Him. He has the power to cast out those who deny Him into Hell. But, for those who believe in Jesus? We need not be afraid because the good news is that God knows us and He cares for us even more than the sparrows that He provides for daily.

We are so precious to God and He cares about every aspect of our lives. He wants us to know Him and rely on Him when times get tough. When my sweet little blond baby boy was eight, he had a health scare and we memorized this scripture together. When he was twenty-four, we finally found answers. God was faithful to us through it all and I believe every word of this verse. Even today when troubles come, I will say this verse over and over again, "Even the very hairs of my head are all numbered. I am worth more than many sparrows."

What is your scripture? What comes into your head when life gets rough? If you don't have a verse you go to,

WEEK 3, DAY 4

let me encourage you to find one that brings God to the forefront of your battle. Let the Lord guide you through the turbulent times and comfort you in His loving arms. Our God is alive and active in our world. He is there with you in every moment. If you cling to Him in the good times, the dark days are never quite as awful. He brings light and hope into every dark space! With God we have nothing to fear!

Today, find a scripture to meditate upon. May it fill your day with comfort and Love! Nothing is too big for God and He rejoices with us in the good times and brings comfort to us in the bad! We are His children, and He loves us infinitely more than we can ever imagine!

Lord, we thank You for guarding over us in our battles in this life. We are so thankful we are not alone and that You care so deeply for us. May we remember to let go and let You fight our battles, while we rest in the comfort of Your loving arms. Thank You for knowing every hair on our head and every need we have ... You are such a gracious and loving Father! In Jesus' Name, amen.

Week 3, Day 5
Nestle In

"If you remain in me and my words remain in you, ask whatever you wish, and it will be given to you."
John 15:7

Russian nesting dolls, or Matryoshka Nesting Dolls as they are known in Russia, are such curious little things. They were created in the late 1800s by a woodworker that depicted the face of a peasant woman on a wooden doll. The dolls were hand painted, each with its own unique features, and fit snuggly one into the other from large to very small. I once sat in a class where this was used as an illustration of John 15:7. Just as these dolls fit one inside the other, we too fit inside Jesus through our faith in Him.

I can visualize Jesus and the Holy Spirit nested together inside of me. If I allow the Word of the Lord to dwell inside of me (smallest doll), letting the Holy Spirit guide and teach me (next doll), and I live out His Will (even bigger doll), I can bear fruit and become more and more like Jesus (bigger doll). As this happens, my prayer life will also be more

WEEK 3, DAY 5

aligned with the Lord (another size up) and will subsequently be more conformed to the will of the Father (even bigger doll). Once we align ourselves with the Will of the Father, we will find ourselves living the blessed life the Father wants to give us, and will be Spirit-led (yep another size up doll). All of this will allow us to pray effective prayers to the Lord that He will grant to us graciously (finally the largest of the nesting dolls).

Just as the nesting dolls fit into each other, we will be able to allow the Holy Spirit to live inside of us and ultimately be connected to the Father. Useful as this analogy is, I know that the Lord God is so Great He could never be contained in a box or as in this case ... a nesting doll! A blessed and productive Spiritual life is our aim, and I love that He lives in me and my hope is that I bear much fruit!

Living as a productive Christian requires a less-of-me, more-of-Him attitude. To bear good fruit for the Kingdom, we must lay down our own selfish wants, and open ourselves up to God's Will. Instead of feeling impatience and frustration, we will begin enjoying the fruit of the Spirit: peace, love, joy, patience, goodness, kindness, faithfulness, gentleness, and self-control as is found in Galatians 5:22-23. Just as the nesting dolls fit perfectly together, our prayer life will fit perfectly together in the Will of our Father. Wow! We are allowed to serve the Kingdom through Christ, following the leading of the Holy Spirit for our God Almighty.

When reading this verse, it is important to note that asking for anything you wish is not an open invitation to ask for anything and expect the Father to immediately grant our requests. This whole verse is about asking for anything that has Kingdom purpose for its advancement. We should

NESTLE IN

be following the guidance of the Holy Spirit and bearing the fruit of the Spirit. With this in mind, we should be praying, listening and obeying. Of course, God wants us to pray without ceasing and to bring Him all our cares and worries but this verse is calling us into His service, and He will answer our prayers! We need that patience and faithfulness here!

Sometimes we think we are following His Will, but our prayers seemingly go unanswered. For example, we might pray for a certain person or ministry that we feel falls into His Kingdom plan as we see it but it didn't work out the way we wanted. Well, we have to remember that we have free will. God will never force any one to accept Him. Therefore, we can present our request to the Lord but the person or thing we are praying for may not respond. Maybe it isn't the right time, or we aren't ready or the person isn't willing.

Disappointing as it can be, what we know is that spreading the gospel is commanded to us, and the Holy Spirit will work through our efforts whether the outcome is as expected or not. One mission field may look completely different from another, so it is important not to compare the fruit we bear with that of another fellow Christian. Just like the nesting dolls fit each inside the other and are protected by the mother doll, we need to nest our faith in Christ, letting the Holy Spirit guide us. Each fits into the next perfectly. All we need to do is diligently obey!

Today, may our hearts be filled with the Spirit, may we pray for opportunities to bear the fruit of the Spirit, and may we be blessed as we go throughout our day! Let us work diligently for as long as there is light, and may we listen for the Spirit to guide us!

WEEK 3, DAY 5

Lord, help us to remain in You through Jesus and Your Word, and may our prayer life be in alignment with Your Kingdom purpose. We are so thankful we can come before Your throne in prayer. Let us always nest ourselves within the confines of Your Will. May we be sensitive to Your guidance as we live out our kingdom lives here on earth. We thank You for hearing us and loving us! In Jesus' Name, amen.

Week 3, Day 6
Help Me!

*... the Spirit helps us in our weakness.
We do not know what we ought to pray,
but the Spirit himself intercedes for us
with groans that words cannot express.*
Romans 8:26

In my first year out of college I moved from a small town into a big city. I had a roommate and together we got acclimated to city life. We were both young girls but we had a free membership to a gym and decided to use it.

My friend began her workout while I began mine and she started hearing this strange guttural noise. Soon she realized everyone was looking at someone, so she turned around with great trepidation. Well, if you haven't guessed already, it was me! I had picked up the bar with no weights because I knew I was not very strong. I groaned and grunted to no avail, and she had to come over and take the bar off of me. At this point she grabs my hand and pulls me out of the gym. We were both laughing hysterically, and she was just mortified.

WEEK 3, DAY 6

I was so glad she was there with me because I honestly don't know how I would've escaped that situation without some very needed help. Well, needless to say, our workouts from that point onward became video tapes in the living room usually ending up with her working out and me watching her while enjoying a bag of chips! But I was there if she needed a helping hand!

Our verse in Romans 8:26 speaks on this subject of helping us out in times of weakness. There are just times where we feel completely helpless. We turn to the Lord in prayer and words just cannot describe the situation adequately. Sometimes we feel like we are praying rubber prayers; you know, the kind you pray and it feels like it is just bouncing off the ceiling. Well, when I get into this kind of a prayer rut, I can turn to the Spirit. This verse calls to me and I pray fervently, "I have no idea what to pray and how to handle this situation, so Holy Spirit please speak to the Father with my needs."

It is such a comfort to have the Holy Spirit with me at all times; especially when the floor has dropped out from under me. I do sometimes ask the Holy Spirit to intercede for me just in case I am needing prayers for something that isn't in the forefront of my mind. It is a beautiful thing to know the Holy Spirit lives within me and is a precious and Holy gift from Jesus. He has entrusted us with the Holy Spirit until He returns, and for that reason alone we should always be looking for His guidance whether in prayer or that gentle nudge we sometimes get.

Does any particular situation come to mind when you have relied on the Holy Spirit to intercede for you? As we stumble through life here on earth, it is sometimes a very

HELP ME!

rocky path to traverse. I love that I am not alone. I love that Jesus gave us the Holy Spirit to live within us and guide us and intercede to the Father for us.

Today, as you pray, ask the Holy Spirit to not only guide your prayers but to intercede on your behalf. Pray the scriptures and listen for the blessings the Father above grants graciously to us.

Lord God Almighty, sometimes life feels completely out of control. We get bogged down by problems at times and need help with asking for the right things. Thank You for the Holy Spirit and I ask that He would intercede for us right now, Lord. Let us be diligent about our prayer life and in being sensitive to the Holy Spirit's promptings. Prayer is powerful, and I am so thankful we are able to come before You with all our cares. In Jesus' Name, amen.

Week 4
SHOW AND TELL

When God created us, He made sure we had our eyes, ears, noses and, of course, mouths! Most of us LOVE to talk. We love to share about places we've visited, people we've met, and exciting stories to amuse and teach. Think on your life and where you have been. Which story in your life do you love to tell? I hope it's a God moment. That's such a natural way to share your faith.

The Old and New Testament are filled with interactions between man and God since the beginning of time. Just because your story isn't featured in the bible doesn't make it any less impactful. This week make time to share your faith story with someone!

Week 4, Day 1
Popping In

For we are to God the aroma of Christ among those who are being saved and those who are perishing.
2 Corinthians 2:15

Close your eyes and imagine yourself walking into a movie theater. What do you hear? What do you smell? What stands out to you? If someone blindfolded you, led you there, and didn't tell you where you were, would you know just by the smell that you were in the lobby of a movie theater?

The aroma of freshly popped popcorn can permeate an entire room, no matter the size. It's an alluring odor, warm and buttery, completely irresistible. Spoiler alert: it's not even really butter. It's a chemical mixture of salt, butter flavor, yellow dye and soy oil that lets off that incredible, buttery smell. But that intoxicating aroma of warm, buttery popcorn that draws you near and makes your mouth water is nothing more than a chemical mixture of something called butter flavor. This smell is so incredibly powerful, yet only mimics the real thing. I'd like to say knowing this helps me

WEEK 4, DAY 1

refrain from eating it but it does not! It's just too enticing to me.

Now, if this popcorn gets burned that's a whole different story. Do the words acrid, pungent or caustic come to mind? Awful doesn't even come close and I immediately get away from that smell.

I think of Satan here where he lures us in to things that make us feel good, smell good, taste good until—we get burned. He hides within a façade of greatness; but in reality is nothing more than evil. Just like the popcorn oil. It smells like the real thing but is really just a chemical.

We as Christians want to influence people to draw near to God. We want to waft an aroma so pure and lovely they want to know where it came from. They want what we have. For this to happen, it needs to be real! No imitation here! This in turn will be a powerful perfume that rises to heaven as we worship and devote ourselves to Christ. We emit a pleasing aroma to God. As for those who are perishing and exude the smell of burnt popcorn, they will one day wish they had never followed the great deceiver.

As a follower of Christ, isn't it lovely to know we are wafting out the fragrance of Christ's love and mercy. How many times are we asked by people to pray for something because they know we are Christians or confide in us because we are known as trustworthy? Just as that enticing smell of popcorn draws us in, so are we able to draw in others to Christ through His love lived out through our actions. Those who are against God will conversely be repelled and sadly, there will always be those that want nothing to do with Christ and have no idea that they exude the smell of death to God.

POPPING IN

Think of your time with God, your actions when you are out in the world, your attitude, your worship, your work environment, what is the aroma you exude? Is your life sending forth a pleasing incense to God? Do you leave that sweet smell of Christ everywhere you go?

Today, as you go about your day, notice the fragrances of your life ... in the office, in your car, in your home and let that perfume remind you that your fragrance might be the aroma of Christ to someone. Ask the Lord in prayer and petition that we exude that alluring bouquet of Christ and give thanks for all He has done. I think today might be a great day to pop in for some popcorn!

Lord God, we praise Your Holy Name! We thank You for Jesus and pray that all our acts of sacrificial worship are a pleasing aroma to You. We pray that we exude a sweet fragrance of Christ's love to the world. In Jesus' Name, amen.

Week 4, Day 2
Too Good Not to Share

That which was from the beginning, which we have heard, which we have seen without eyes, which we have looked at and our hands have touched—this we proclaim concerning the Word of life.
1 John 1:1

I have always been a very tactile person. I feel almost everything I see. I was surprised to learn that our sense of touch is the first thing to develop in humans. This sense of touch is so acute that our fingers can feel a bump just one micron high (a micron is one-millionth of a meter). This is completely undetectable to the human eye! Sit for a second and think of your favorite things to touch—soft rose petals, sugary sand, a baby's downy hair or a smooth blade of grass. The list is probably endless as there are so many things we touch continuously. We can feel things that we cannot even see, ah-mazing!

Now imagine if you can, being able to physically touch or hug Jesus. Let's rest here a minute. I don't see myself shaking His hand but delicately reaching out to touch His arm. Just thinking about that brings chill bumps to me. In our passage in John, these men were able to not only hear Jesus speak, and look at Him in human form but to touch Him and most likely hug Him. When these men proclaimed the Word of Life, it was real. They were close friends with Jesus. Their testimony was powerful and is still being read by us today. These men were hugged by the Almighty God in human form!

Praise the Lord we get to feel the Spirit of God move deep within our souls! When the Holy Spirit moves, nothing on earth can compare to that indescribable feeling.

When we experience something wonderful, how many of us keep it to ourselves? Everyone has a story they have told over and over to many different audiences. Is your story Jesus? Does your story impact others? There are things that happen in our lives that we KNOW are nothing short of God's hand upon our lives. I do have a story; I have many stories but there is one particular event I experienced such an amazing intervention of God. My youngest son contracted RSV at two and half weeks old. My baby was turning blue, was shivering just to grab a little air. He took in so little air, however, he couldn't even cry. We had already been to the ER and in utter terror I looked up to the ceiling and simply said HELP! I watched my little guy's body relax as he took in a huge gulp of air. From this point forward he breathed in and out normally. I was front row center to a miracle of God. There is no other explanation, and I will tell this story until the day I die. Praise the Lord for His mercy and for the opportunity to share His love and care for me and my family.

WEEK 4, DAY 2

I praise God that these men were able to share in Jesus' life and ministry. I am thankful that they were able to see, hear and feel the one and only Jesus. They were first on the scene and some wrote their experiences. No matter how they communicated their interactions with Christ, they did not walk away quietly but joyously shared the good news of Jesus. So, how have you felt God in your life and what is your story?

Today, be thankful to God for His Holy Spirit that dwells inside us. Praise God we are able to experience Him in such an intimate way! Remember your God story and share it! God is alive, Jesus is alive, and the Holy Spirit is alive! The Godhead is with us and has touched our lives. Let's proclaim His Living Word every chance we get! There is really nothing out there that compares to His touch!

Lord, we are so amazed at all the ways You move in our lives. You are a personal Savior to each one of us and interact with us throughout our lives. Lord, may we be bold enough to share our testimony of faith with all we meet. Thank You for being our God! In Jesus' Name, amen.

Week 4, Day 3
Game On

But the fruit of the Spirit is love, joy, peace, patience, kindness, goodness, faithfulness, gentleness and self-control. Against such things there is no law.
Galatians 5:22-23

Have you heard the one about the Christian lady who went to the grocery store? Well, I hope not because this isn't one of my finest moments. You see, I like to do my shopping on days that aren't too crowded, so I can saunter around without causing others to have to wait for me. Otherwise, when the store is busy it plays out a lot like a football game with me vs. everyone else.

Today was one of the football days at the store because apparently it was a school holiday. I decided I was going to be healthy and eat fresh fruit and vegetables, and maybe lose a few of those stubborn pounds that have landed on my hips. I park and head into the store feeling pretty good, joyful even. I see a cart not in the bin. so, I grab it, saving a bumper and another parking place, A+ I'm thinking. I knew

WEEK 4, DAY 3

I would only be in the fruit and veggies area, so this will be a quick trip in and out!

However, on my way in, my husband calls and wants something that will detour me to the back of the store. Once inside, it's a flurry of activity. Moms, dads and children of all ages everywhere. I'm shocked at this as I head back to the dairy area. Well, game on, I think to myself.

Here's the play by play. As I come up to the line of scrimmage (packed main aisle), I survey the defense (shoppers) looking for a weak spot to exploit. As I come upon an obstacle (very slow shopper), I fake left and go right but so does she, tackled for no gain. Next play, I see a hole in the defense, so I call a quick audible and run the cart to the eggs. Touchdown! I got the eggs. Now time for the extra point—the fruit and veggie aisle. I put on my game face and run a sweep towards the meat aisle, which is halfway to my destination. The cart is in play and the crowd is going wild ... it's pandemonium because another three carts are coming in for the stop! So now I speed up and weave left and head into the end zone (fruit and veggie area). Needless to say, my joy is gone, and I am extremely frustrated.

So, I'm waiting at the lemons and a lady says, "Oh I'm so sorry." I smile, grit my teeth and respond, "No problem." This has been a tough battlefield and I'm bloody and bruised. I need an attitude adjustment, so it's time to leave the gridiron and enter back into the fruit-filled life that I am supposed to be living. This lady and I strike up a conversation and as I cool off, I realize this lady is oozing the fruit of the Spirit. Am I? I ran into yet another lady and I moved aside to let her go first as I worked to get a bag open. She looked at me and smiled and said, "Prayer works!"

GAME ON

Never was a word more impactful than at that moment! Touchdown for her!

Galatians 5 is such an easy thing to do when you aren't on the playing field. Love, joy, peace, patience, gentleness etc. seems a recipe to get beaten down. But that's the thing about living a victorious life through Jesus. He's already won the game. We aren't here to beat down the opposition but to lead others onto the winning team. Jesus is the ultimate quarterback, tight end, defensive end and kicker! He alone can take the ball for us. We need to be living out a fruit-filled life and we will be on the winning Super Bowl team!

The fruit and veggie aisle was exactly where I needed to be. Not only did I find my fruit and veggies but I found I needed to throw some fruit of the Spirit into my cart as well. So what happened? Well, I'd let ME get in the way. Everything became about me. Who is making me wait? Who is in my way? Whose kids are these that are running all around me? In Ephesians 5:1, we are told to be imitators of God and in Philippians 2:3 we are told to do nothing out of selfish ambition. How can I be Jesus to others without loving others and putting them ahead of myself? I need to be acting on what the Spirit of the Lord tells me, and I'll certainly know if I'm not following His lead. How? Our verse in Galatians gives a good guideline of how we need to be acting with love, joy, peace, patience, kindness, goodness, faithfulness, gentleness and self-control.

Well, today I was humbled and thankful that He kept me in step with the Holy Spirit. An innocuous trip to the store became a football game where I was fighting through the opponent when I needed to just take a knee and let Jesus take over.

WEEK 4, DAY 3

Today, let us infuse ourselves in the Word of God. Let the fruit of the Spirit be characterized by the way we treat others and by our attitude. I think I am going to go eat an apple and spend a little time reading His playbook!

Lord God, we ask to be infused with the power of the Holy Spirit. Let our lives be filled with all the fruit of the Spirit as we strive to be more and more like Christ. Help us to be Jesus to everyone we encounter today! In Jesus' Name, amen.

Week 4, Day 4
A Little More Salt, Please

Let your conversation be always full of grace,
seasoned with salt, so that you may know
how to answer everyone.
Colossians 4:6

Have you ever eaten a meal without any salt at all? Have you ever been cooking and knew the dish was not quite right, only to find more salt fixed the issue? Salt brings a depth of flavor to our food as well as preserves our food. Too much salt is never a good thing though and many of us salt-a-holics need to beware. The average American diet is, unfortunately, super high in sodium and it isn't coming from just our own salt shakers. It is loaded into so many of the foods that line our shelves and hang out in our refrigerators and freezers. This is one of the components that make it taste so yummy! Just as salt preserves and enhances the flavor of our food, it also is used as an example for our speech in Colossians.

Many instances in the bible use salt as an illustration

WEEK 4, DAY 4

because it was such a valuable commodity. Salt was essential for life back then because it had more uses than just a food flavoring. Salt in biblical days preserved their food, was used as a cleanser, and was even used medicinally. Salt was also used in temple offerings, so it is apparent that salt would make a great symbol to use in teaching during biblical times.

Today, we will anchor here in Colossians 4 where Paul is exhorting us to let our words reflect Christ in our lives. If someone said my words were salty or that I had salty language I never would have translated it to mean it was filled with grace.

Today, if our daily conversations and actions are full of love and the Will of Christ, we will stand out as different, and as people to be respected. When we radiate Christ in our lives, we have added salt to our words, and placed Him right in the center of our conversations. In your everyday life, do you find yourself telling people you will pray for them? Do you find yourself dropping Jesus' name? Are you known for clean language? Ephesians 4:29 goes quite well with our Colossians verse today. In Ephesians we are told not to let any unwholesome talk come out of our mouths. I believe this includes not only what we say but the topics as well.

When we are spoken of, we want our language to be representative of Jesus. When we speak, we do not want to be spreading gossip or malicious intent. Isn't it nice when people realize we are Christian just because of our daily conversations? We not only impact them as being loving, trustworthy and positive people, we are a living example of Christ dwelling in our daily lives.

Today, let's be prepared for the divine and life-changing

moments where we can share our faith or be asked to pray for someone or something. Just as we sprinkle our food with salt, may we sprinkle our conversations with His sweet Spirit.

Lord God, we thank You for the opportunities to be Your ambassador to this world. We ask that our speech be pure and full of You. Open doors for us to spread Your love through our words and actions. There is nothing better in this life than to spend it knowing we are saved through the blood of Christ, and we are blessed to be able to share this Good News! In Jesus' precious Name, amen.

Week 4, Day 5
Let Love Shine!

Yet I am writing you a new command; its truth is seen in him and you, because the darkness is passing and the true light is already shining.
1 John 2:8

Of all the lights in the sky—the sun, moon, and stars—one of them brings me such joy to see. It's the harvest moon, so named because it is the last full moon of the summer season or the first full moon at the beginning of Fall. Closest to fall, it signifies the time to harvest the summer crops such as corn. This full, almost orange moon floods the night sky with the light the farmers would need to get all their crops harvested past sunset. I'm not sure how much work the farmers would get out of me because I find that magnificent moon mesmerizing. When the moon is heavy and low before it reaches its full height, I cannot look away. I love how it illuminates the darkness with its buttery brilliance.

In the same way, John the apostle writes of the true light: Jesus. As Jesus walked the earth, His divine splendor shone everywhere He went. No one who came into His presence left unchanged, even those who meant Him harm. His light permeated even the darkest of souls, illuminating their true selves. His eternal light is shining through us all into the darkness of our world. The more depraved the world becomes, the brighter His light shines.

When John writes of the darkness passing and the true Light shining. it makes me think of that beautiful Harvest Moon. It illuminates the darkness, relieving us of the blackness that makes us fear each step. As we grow and mature in our faith, our light will begin to shine bright and illuminate the murkiness around us. The darker the world becomes, the greater our light will shine in contrast.

One day, there will be no more darkness. Revelation 21:5 says that we will have no more need for the sun or the moon or a lamp because the Lord God will give us light. Wow, I can't even imagine the splendor that awaits us in heaven!

Imagining this new heaven and new earth described in Revelation 21 is more than my human mind can comprehend. In verse 25 it states there will be no night there. The radiance of the Father will be our light! In Revelation 22, the last chapter of the bible, John speaks of the angel showing him the river of life, crystal clear water that flows from the throne of God and the Lamb. Oh how amazing it will be to see the reflection of His True Light off of the golden streets and sparkling waters!

Today, meditate on the light Jesus shines from within you. Make an effort to walk outside tonight and admire the moon. Be it a full moon or a sliver, it still radiates light from above to illuminate the inky darkness. Let His Light flood our very being so that we radiate His goodness and

WEEK 4, DAY 5

love everywhere we go! May His light be so bright that it brings others to know Him too! Let's reflect His Light just as the Harvest Moon brightens up the night, dispelling the darkness for the harvesters to see and work!

Lord God, thank You so much for the Harvest Moon. It shines so bright and is so glorious that we just cannot look away. Let the light from the moon remind us to let Your light shine through us continuously. Let us remember that the harvest is at hand, so we need to spread Your radiance to every single person You put in our paths. In Jesus' Name, amen.

Week 4, Day 6
Wrap Me Up

After that, He poured water into a basin and began to wash his disciples' feet, drying them with the towel that was wrapped around him.
John 13:5

I know most people prefer a shower, but I love nothing more than a long soak in a nice, hot bathtub. There is nothing like that squeaky clean feeling. I proceed to wrap up in a clean, thick, warm towel and dry off all the water. I do this every night as part of my ritual to relax and prepare for bed. We may take for granted our modern-day luxuries, but I am grateful for my bathtub and fluffy towels.

Our modern-day towels didn't look quite like those in Jesus' day. The towel we know today began in Bursa, Turkey, but before this time, towels were made from strips of linen. I'm sure they were rough and scratchy and could use some good fabric softener. But, hey, they got the job done!

In our verse today, we see Jesus wrapping a towel around His waist as He began a chore that was traditionally done by

WEEK 4, DAY 6

servants or women. The washing of feet was a menial task and done as an act of hospitality to guests. Because of the terrain and the fact that the travelers wore sandals, washing their feet also helped them to relax and prepare for their meal. This meal was a special meal, The Last Supper.

As the disciples reclined around the table with their Teacher, they knew how important He was. The action of Jesus in this moment demonstrated major humility. In Luke 22:23-24, we read of the men arguing over who would be greatest in heaven. Meanwhile, you have Jesus wrapping Himself in a towel about to wash their dirty feet. While the disciples are showing selfish ambition and pride, here is Jesus demonstrating complete selfless humility.

Are we wrapping ourselves in a towel of pride or a towel of humility? Jesus was a server. His entire ministry here on earth demonstrated time and again of Who He Was and What He Was About. It's not about our title at church. It's not about our puffed-up egos or how talented we are, no, His ministry focused on loving others and putting others ahead of Himself.

Today, read John 13 from the perspective of Jesus' disciples. Read this chapter with the realization that Jesus is God in human flesh. Think about the precedent He has set. How can we follow His example? Let's look for ways to love and be a servant to others. When we reach for a towel today, let it be a reminder to humbly serve others at every opportunity given.

Lord God, what an example Jesus is to us! The Son of the most Holy, not only lowered Himself to be a human walking this earth, but He also became a servant to those around Him. Let us look to Jesus as an example, and help us to serve others with a grateful heart. In Jesus' Name, amen.

Week 5
TITHE, REST AND WORK

Oh, living the Christian life can be such a blessing! God created us perfectly so we could perform the tasks set before us. With all the time, money and talents He has given us, He still wants our first fruits to be given to Him. We need to give Him off the top, not the leftovers. Everything from our work to our ministries to even our Sunday afternoon rest should be done with the right heart of obedience to God.

    Take the time this week to do some self-reflection on what God has done for you. Think about the gifts He has lavished on you. Even the time He has given for rest is a gift from Him. Do you take advantage of rest or do you fill every space with more work? Do the tithes you set aside show your reliance on Him? This week let us be reminded that <u>everything</u> we have is a gift from Him. Thank Him continuously for His provision. We are so blessed!

Week 5, Day 1
Determined Life of a Turtle

Whatever you do, work heartily,
as for the Lord and not for men.
Colossians 3:23 ESV

Sea turtles I found out are quite abundant on the beaches in Hawaii. I have never seen so many in one place in my life! We came upon a beach that was nothing but green sea turtles. There were so many, it looked like a polka dotted beach! They are such patient, hard-working creatures! We watched them ride the waves until they hit the ground and then patiently waited for the wave to pop them up on the beach. From this point, they made their arduous journey up the beach until they found a free space to sun with their friends. I wondered why they would leave the ease of their watery home to struggle on to this sandy beach. I knew they laid their eggs on shore, but this was not the case. So, I researched and found they do this for rest, heat and safety.

Under the sea, they are such elegant and graceful creatures. On land they are chubby, slow, and unsteady.

WEEK 5, DAY 1

It almost hurt me to watch them wobble at every step. I would too if I weighed over 400 lbs. and had flippers for feet to traverse the shifting sand. But, hey, I didn't hear even one complaint!

I think about this verse in Colossians and how applicable it is to the way the sea turtles live their lives. We are instructed to give our all to everything we do just as if the Lord had asked us to do it. How many times do we get caught up in the mundane tasks of the day and do not have our hearts in it? We basically go through the motions, struggling through our day as if we have a turtle shell on our back. God understands life is hard, but He instructs us to work hard and with integrity. After all, our talent to do the job, whether for personal income or volunteer work, is provided to us by God. In turn, we need to happily give Him 100%!

When we work as if for the Lord, we find our attitude changes. We are working with purpose, and at the end of the day feel like we have accomplished something that God has called us to do. When the time comes to retire from your job, wouldn't it be great to look back and see how hard you worked and how God has blessed you throughout the years? Let's be like those giant sea turtles with their heavy shells that struggle to get to the sandy expanse to warm up and be protected. They live their lives without complaint, and as they make their way back to their watery home where they glide effortlessly through the deep, they know that cumbersome shell is their protection. Let's work hard to give glory to God with humility and strength of character and let Him carry our heavy burdens.

Today, as we go about our day, let us live out our Christ-filled life and not grow weary but with thanks and praise, work as if we are working for the Lord. Let us not feel weighed down and give in to laziness or grumbling. May we have the strength and determination of those sweet, humble, green sea turtles!

Lord God, we praise You for Your provisions in our lives. We thank You for the talents and opportunities You have given us so that we might live a life of active obedience. Let us never tire of the work put before us but let us persevere and give it our all. May we bring glory to You always! Everything we have, including our jobs, is from You! Let us live our lives in a way that is pleasing and brings honor to You. In Jesus' Name, amen.

Week 5, Day 2
Work Like a Dog

I know that there is nothing better for men than to be happy and do good while they live. That every man may eat and drink and find satisfaction in all his toil—this is the gift of God.
Ecclesiastes 3:12-13

When my kids were young, they loved reading this book they found about a K-9 dog. The book explained how this K-9 loved going to work; but when he was off duty, he was just a happy, regular member of his master's family. Once the K-9 vest came out, this dog would immediately pep up and get serious. He had a sense of purpose and was happy to give it everything in his sweet heart to serve and protect his owner. K-9s originated in the late 1800s, so those lucky enough to be chosen and trained were able to happily go to work with their owner and are still doing so today. It seems these dogs are the perfect example of this scripture in Ecclesiastes.

While not all of us love our jobs, work is essential for living. Think about this verse in Ecclesiastes 3. God wants us to live morally, and He does not want us to be lazy. He wants us to work hard. We tend to more fully appreciate what we have because we know we earned it. He wants us to feel the satisfaction of a job well done. When we work and live in such a way, this is a blessing not only for ourselves but also because we are pleasing God. We stand out to those around us whose toil is not done with a kingdom compass.

Have you worked alongside people whose heart just isn't in their job? It is disheartening to have to listen to them complain or pick up the slack when they didn't finish their work or did it sloppily. Once the workday is over, isn't it interesting how the complaining doesn't stop? Compare the thankful attitude to the negative attitude ... and now ... reread the last sentence in our scripture. Which do we fuel? The discontent of our lives or the contentedness of being thankful for what God has given us?

Being joyfully content and thankful, and dedicated to giving it our all will make our tasks less difficult. If we give in to idleness or procrastination, we find ourselves fueling discontent. Let's propel ourselves to work hard and feel satisfaction. Like the K-9, we should be happy to take on all the challenges of the day. It feels as if we made a difference, even if only in our little world, and will rest better at the end of a productive day.

Today, let us work like the K-9! After all, work and rest are gifts from God!

Lord God, let us come before You and give thanks for all the opportunities we have to work hard for You. You have placed us right where You want us, so we may work hard and serve You in everything we do. Let our attitude be joyful and our hearts be engaged as we go throughout our day. In Jesus' Name, amen.

Week 5, Day 3
Happy Trails

*Clear a level path for your feet,
so all your ways will be firm.*
Proverbs 4:26 TLV

I love nature trails. It's just like I've stepped into another world. With each step, I hear and feel the crunching of leaves and twigs, I hear the birds chirping and the rustling of deer. I walk in the shade of the trees enjoying the dappled sunlight as it breaks through every so often. Then, when I am hot and weary from my trek, a gentle wind blows through; a most refreshing feeling. I stop to quench my thirst with a cool drink of water and oh how sweet that water is! Dead in my tracks I find myself basking in the splendor of the forest. Right there in my utopia, I am encapsulated by nature. I never know what I may stumble upon but one thing I know for sure is to stay on the marked trail! And off I go again!

The one thing I have learned through hiking with my family is to never—no matter how enticing—never, leave the marked trail. We are given a map with clearly defined and safe passages that are maintained by the rangers. I know it can appear safe traipsing through the trees thinking we can walk in and find our way out; but that is not always the case. There's a reason we are instructed not to stray even if we cannot see the danger. Any number of animals, ledges, holes and even unseen dangers could prove disastrous. Do you trust and obey the powers that be to keep you safe or are you a rebel and veer off the tried and true paths? The level paths? The firm paths?

I love to imagine my Christian walk as I do a hiking trail, with Jesus as my trail guide and the bible as my map. He has so much to teach and show me. All I need to do is to stay on the right path and read my map, the Bible, daily. That can be easier said than done. It is important that we consider everything we do in our lives carefully. We have so many choices, and it is important that our words, thoughts, actions and feet are aligned with Christ. It can be easy to be lured off our path but the goal is to follow where He leads us. Why? Because out of all the many exciting avenues we can choose to pursue in this life, only one leads to Him and His eternal life. It is so important that we know and trust our "trail guide" so we can experience all the wonders of this world. His Way is level and firm and, although it's not always easy, it's filled with blessings.

In Proverbs 4, the path that is mentioned here is not a physical but a spiritual one. The Lord God is eager to bless us as we journey through our lives, but we must carefully and deliberately stay with our guide (the Holy Spirit) and use our map (the Holy Bible). This will require us to do more than just live moral lives. We need to sacrificially and obediently follow Him wherever He leads us. With our bible not

WEEK 5, DAY 3

only do we have a map to guide us but a way to know our Guide intimately. Through prayer and the movement of the Holy Spirit we are protected and directed through the trials and pitfalls of this life. Does the word "trust" flash through your mind? It's okay that it's hard to do sometimes, and we all struggle with that one thing. But it is essential to trust God and take comfort from knowing our Lord walks alongside us to guide and protect us. Let go and let God take the lead. All our walks in this life will look different. Some will have hard places to traverse but the bible assures us we won't walk alone. My soul swells with love and gratitude for all He does for us! What a beautiful way to live!

Today, ask yourself what path you are on, and ask the Lord to guide you on the path of eternal Life. May we find complete and utter joy in serving the Lord! Walking with Him is an adventure full of amazing places and people to see! Thank the Lord continually for guiding us on our daily walk with Him. Ask Him for His guidance in tough times, and for the wisdom to navigate the way He leads us.

Lord, we thank You for walking with us today. We pray that we heed Your voice and follow Your guidance, so we do not take the wrong path. We are thankful that You are there at every turn and that if we do get lost, You are there to get us back on track! In Jesus' Name, amen.

Week 5, Day 4
Slow Your Roll!

Then God blessed the seventh day and made it holy, because on it he rested from all the work of creating that he had done.
Genesis 2:3

Once church is done, lunch is eaten and I am back home relaxing, there is nothing quite like that Sunday afternoon nap. On Sunday there is a different feeling when I rest. There is no guilt or feeling that I am wasting my day when I could be productive somewhere else. Even if I don't sleep, Sunday is spent resting and enjoying time with the friends and family that God has blessed me with. Sunday is the sabbath for me but the Jewish sabbath is observed on Saturday. The word sabbath means rest and God felt it was so important for man to rest that He not only demonstrated this in Genesis, but also commanded it to be observed by the Jewish people.

Our days are filled with activity and work. The busier we are, the more difficult it seems to stop and rest. Our

WEEK 5, DAY 4

minds are constantly going with our increasing dependence on phones and computers. How many times do we head to bed, and our brains just cannot shut down? I have noticed even my focus is not as strong as it was before I had instant access to everything via my computer. Resting and setting aside a time to recharge our bodies is therefore essential not only to our health but to pleasing God. He wants us to work but He also knows we need to rest.

In Jesus' time their days looked very different from ours. Men worked hard out in the fields or fishing or in their trade. The women spent their days hard at work preparing meals, raising their families and supplementing the family income. Their lives were way more physically active than most of ours today. In the Old Testament their day of rest was designated for them in the Ten Commandments, and not only they but their servants and animals were to observe the Sabbath rest (Exodus 23:12).

Setting aside a day of rest is a command from God. On the actual day we rest, we have the opportunity to focus on God and what He has done for us as well as rest our physical bodies. If we have family, it also allows us to spend quality time together. After we have had a day of rest, we are refreshed and ready to work and serve the Lord anew. God created us in His own image, and He knows exactly what is best for us. I am sure if it was a part of the Ten Commandments and then reiterated in the New Testament in Hebrews 4:8-11, it was an intentional command that still holds true today. This passage in Hebrews states that when we enter God's rest, we also rest from our own work. Both the Old and New Testament confirm that we are expected to rest by God. And I do love my Sunday nap!

SLOW YOUR ROLL!

Today, thank God for the work He has given you. If you have a day set aside for your sabbath, thank God for that rest. If today happens to be your day of rest, enjoy and dedicate it to the Lord. If you do not have a set day of rest, it is a great time to rededicate a day to the Lord as your sabbath. Let's slow our roll and obediently take a breather!

Lord God, in this time of never-ending busyness, we celebrate You and honor You as we set aside a sabbath day to rest and recharge. We thank You for our lives as well as the time You have given us to rest. Help us, Lord, to find this day of rest as important as our days of work. To You be the glory forever! Amen.

Week 5, Day 5
God Loves a Good BBQ

*In the course of time Cain brought some of the fruits
of the soil as an offering to the Lord. But Abel brought
fat portions from some of the firstborn of his flock.
The Lord looked with favor on Abel and his offering.*
Genesis 4:3-4

I have this dear friend from South Africa. Her sweet voice and accent is precious and I love to listen to her speak. Once, while we were sitting around my kitchen table talking about different things we love, she mentioned her love for the smell of grilled meat fat in her awesome South African tenor. Hmmm, grilled meat fat? I sat for a second thinking and then said, "You mean BBQ"?

"Yep, BBQ!"

She told me it made her think of the meat offerings that were given to the Lord. As we talked about it, she stopped and said, "I told my husband, I guess God loves barbecue too." Well, that was priceless and yet so true. We don't have to read far into our bible to find where it speaks of God's love of BBQ.

GOD LOVES A GOOD BBQ

In the beginning of Genesis is the story of Cain and Abel. It didn't take long for sibling rivalry to show up, did it? Cain worked the soil and Abel worked the flock. Each had an offering to the Lord but Abel's barbecued firstborn offering was the one that pleased God. This certainly didn't go over well with Cain, and so begins the sad story of the first murder committed in history. Now that is taking sibling rivalry to the extreme, I know, but let's focus on the actual issue at hand. Here we have the first firsts; the first sibling rivalry, the first murder, and seemingly, the first documented BBQ! Now, I don't want to make light of this story because God was very serious about the heart of giving. Obviously, Cain's heart was not in the right place. The bible does not tell us at this point what instructions had been set forth to these boys, but we do know from scripture that God asked for the first fruits. So what does God want from us today when it comes to giving Him a pleasing offering? He wants the best, He wants the firsts, and He wants the right attitude of worship and giving.

We see in our verse today that the Lord looked with favor on Abel's offering. Abel wanted to give God the best that he had to give. This is still the gold standard for giving today. When we give to God with the right heart and from the best we have to offer, before even ourselves, He honors that sacrificial giving. The Lord will look with favor on our gift. We can give any manner of ways including money or time or doing without.

God knows our hearts and that giving of our time and money is hard and scary for us. When we give to Him sacrificially, it shows our dedication to and reliance on Him. God in turn will honor us for this giving. Other scriptures

WEEK 5, DAY 5

back this up such as in Malachi 3:10. He says that if we give our tithes to Him with the right heart, He will open the floodgates of heaven with so much blessing we won't have enough room for more. He says here in this passage to test Him in this giving. 2 Corinthians 9:7 also encourages us to give cheerfully what you have decided in your heart to give. This is a true show of love, faith and devotion to our God almighty—a litmus test if you will of where our hearts really lie.

Where is your heart? Who gets the firsts in your life? And what is truly meaningful that you want to give to the Lord? Will it be as acceptable as Abel's gift of the wonderful incense from the fat portions of his flock? God loved His wonderful barbecue because it was given with a heart to please Him.

Today, when you smell that delicious aroma of cooked food ... let it be a reminder that anything we give to God, He will honor if it is done with the right attitude. Let's give to Him off the top, and cheerfully.

Lord God, You are so worthy of all our Firsts. I pray that You will find any offering of our time, money or talents to You acceptable. Lord, forgive us if we have robbed You in any way or have displeased You by not giving with the right heart or assigning You the leftovers. Lord, work with us and help to set us on the right path of giving. Give us the bravery to step out in faith, and trust You with our time and money. In Jesus' Name, amen.

Week 5, Day 6
It All Began with a Leaf

Taste and see that the Lord is good; blessed is the man that takes refuge in him.
Psalm 34:8 ESV

There is nothing more wonderful to me than a good cup of hot tea. Once it passes from my lips, I can almost trace it down my throat into my stomach, like a warm hug from the inside. When there is something that feels so comforting and lovely, we just want to share it with those around us, we just can't help ourselves. So I am always happy to share a hot cup of tea with anyone who comes into my home. I mean, how can I keep such a magical elixir all to myself???

When I think of hot tea I think of Great Britain. The Brits definitely love their tea. However, when I think of medicinal tea, I think of China. Truth be told, the origin of tea lies throughout Asia where it was used as medicine. I often ponder how someone looked at a leaf and thought, let's put this in some hot water and see what happens! I

WEEK 5, DAY 6

don't think I'd be excited to be the first one to actually try it but I guess everything we eat and drink had a guinea pig who tasted it to see if it was safe and yummy. Whoever first drank that first hot cup of tea though opened the door to the wonderful flavors and healing properties of tea that are still enjoyed today! Fascinating how a simple dried leaf can transform plain water into a brandy colored, rich tasting drink with so many health benefits to boot!

Isn't this a great way to think of the Word of God? As we study His Word and discover how much we love and crave the Lord, shouldn't we want to share it with all those around us? Imagine, instead of offering your guests a cup of tea, we offered them a blessing from the Word. His Word will provide a warmth that is eternal. He provides us with a medicine that heals our broken hearts and restores our souls. His love is stronger than anything we find in this world.

A simple blessing spoken to another from the Lord is more powerful than anything we can say. It seeps into our veins and transforms our lives. His Word is alive and active and infuses all who accept and hear His voice with an eternal warmth that flows through our bodies. It is that eternal hope and mercy that propels us to love and obey Him in all we do. Let His divine Word transform us like that simple tea leaf transformed the plain water. Once we are steeped in Him, we will never be the same.

Sit down today with a nice cup of tea and His Holy Word

Taste and see that the Lord is good and let this truth dwell within your soul today. Savor its meaning, and as you dig into His Word, feel the warmth it brings to your soul. There is no other book like it.

IT ALL BEGAN WITH A LEAF

Lord God, we thank You for Your Holy Word. Let us take refuge in You today and every day. May Your Truth fill our cup to the brim, seep into every vein of our body and let us share this cup of wisdom with all we come upon today. In Jesus' Name, amen.

Week 6
PRAISE AND JOY

Have you ever looked around and wondered how anyone could not know there is a God that created this world. Even His creation praises Him through its very existence! The vibrant colors in nature, the powerful winds, the melodious insects and birds, the tenderness seen in the eyes of our pets—I think I could go on forever. Even our songs when belted out in love and adoration for God and Jesus bring an inner joy that simply cannot be explained!

I am so thankful for being able to focus on Him in every aspect of my life. It is so hard not to praise Him when we take the time to consider all He has done and given to us. This week I hope your heart is filled with joy as you find new and revive old ways to praise our Lord!

Week 6, Day 1
Melodies of the Heart

*Shout for joy to the Lord, all the earth. Serve the Lord
with gladness, come before him with joyful songs.*
Psalm 100:1-2 ESV

Music is a precious gift from God. It is such a primal way to express our emotions and soothe our souls. We each have different likes from instrumental to rock and roll. Cue Donny and Marie Osmond. She's a little bit country and he's a little bit rock 'n' roll. Although not every singing voice is quite ready for the music industry, God loves all the voices He created! He also created an inmost love for song deep within us, we were after all created in His own image.

The scriptures that encourage singing and music are referenced over 1,150 times according to insearchoftruth.com. Singing and dancing were found not only in happy times but also in times of mourning. Revelation 11:15 tells us to be listening for the trumpet call and I look forward to hearing the harps in heaven. The book of Psalms is the hymnal of the bible, although examples of song and poetry are interspersed

WEEK 6, DAY 1

throughout the bible. In Ephesians 5:19 we are commanded to sing and make music to the Lord from our hearts.

In today's verse, we are encouraged to shout out to the Lord and praise His Name. Imagine such joy bursting forth from your lungs, stirring your heart so powerfully, your mouth has to open wide and release this emotion in song! Now this is Soul Music!!! This is the way God loves to hear us sing praise and scripture verses to Him. He's like a parent listening to their little ones sing joyfully. I can just imagine His pride and love for us.

So, let us burst out with song and praise to the Lord! Let us notice when our minds capture a scripture we learned through song. Let us intentionally listen to praise music and sing aloud these praises back to the Lord. I've been caught by neighbors singing and dancing to my praise music as I garden. I've been known to hold a concert in my car and look and see someone looking in with a smile ... if they only knew for Whom I am singing! I hope they felt the joy of my heart without ever hearing my voice. I know this morning as I woke up, my inner jukebox was playing the song "Great are you, Lord." I love how praise music just exudes from my heart all day long! Oh, the joy it brings to the soul!

Today, make time to sing to the Lord even if it's just in your head and heart. The Lord hears our every thought as well as every word we speak. Sing with all your might—in the car or at home; dance for Him and praise Him all through the day.

Lord God, I am so thankful for the melodies that bring me closer to You. Music brings joy to my soul and helps me remember Your Word. May my voice bring praise and honor to You! In Jesus' Name, amen.

Week 6, Day 2
Oh, What a Relief!

Rejoice in the Lord always. I will say it again. Rejoice!
Philippians 4:4

As summer begins to wane here in the South everything seems to breathe a collective sigh of relief. Soon we begin to feel the world around us start to change. Sure, we still get a lot of Indian summers but there's that one day the wind picks up and a wonderful cool breeze washes over us. The leaves begin to turn from their scorched green leaves to the brilliant colors of red, gold and orange. Now these leaves are dancing in the wind until they fall off and waft onto the ground below.

Meanwhile, even the animals sense the change and begin to frolic around in the new cool, breezy season. As the days become shorter and the sunlight wanes, the world around settles into its new rhythms of Fall. Oh, what a joy to feel the cooler days relieve us of the oppressive heat of the summer months! For me this is a time to dance and send praise to the Lord with a very joyful and thankful heart!

WEEK 6, DAY 2

Just as we rejoice over the fresh cool breezes that settle in after the long, balmy summer season, we should eagerly express our joy and gratitude to our Father in Heaven. There is so much to rejoice to the Lord about in our world around us. Our salvation alone is worthy of praise, and everything else around is a bonus. Ponder the changing of the seasons, the care He gives to those who trust in Him, the provision He has for us, and the Love He continually showers upon us. We can take for granted all the blessings that the Lord has bestowed upon us and we need to slow down and be fully present and alert.

In Philippians we are instructed to rejoice in the Lord ALWAYS, and in doing so, we honor the Lord! When? Always. It's so easy to be joyful when our lives are great but what about when we find ourselves in a time of trial? Maybe this joy is an active word ... we actively and purposely change our attitude to focus on joy. Before we know it, our hearts will feel just a little bit lighter, and we can experience a heart of thankfulness and even a sense of peace. We just need to keep our focus on Him.

Everything about the Lord is everlasting and perfect. Even in times of despair, He is still there with us! When we find ourselves in trouble, seek Him and ask what it is we need to learn from this situation. Ask for His joy and peace because of His astounding love and provision. As we emerge from our time of hardship, look back and see how He brought you through your trial. Praise His Holy Name! Imagine the impact you make on the world when your hope is displayed through joy and thankfulness during hardship.

When we slow down and purposefully set our minds on Him with a thankful and joyful heart, how can we not

OH, WHAT A RELIEF!

rejoice? Can you feel His presence? Are you basking in His love? Are you bathing in His Word daily? And does His joy burst from your heart as you think on All He has done for you? Just as nature proclaims its relief from the boiling summer temps to the sweetness of the cool fall days, may we rejoice in the Lord's goodness!

Be it Summer, Spring, Winter or Fall, let Him bathe us in His sweetness and His presence. Feel His love waft over and around us like a gentle wind. Let our soul dance in His inexplicable and immeasurable love, and let the beauty of the world around remind us to rejoice in the Lord and stand in awe of His goodness!

Lord, we thank You for all the seasons in our lives. We rejoice in Your goodness and love, and pray that, whether it's a season of hardship or ease, that we see that You are right here beside us! May we be thankful and rejoice in all situations, for we know You are a good and faithful Father. In Jesus' Name, amen.

Week 6, Day 3
Starry Night

"Blessed be your glorious name, and may it be exalted above all blessing and praise. You alone are the Lord. You made the heavens, even the highest heavens, and all their starry host, the earth and all that is on it, the seas and all that is in them. You give life to everything, and the multitudes of heaven worship you."
Nehemiah 9:5b-6

A memory I hold near and dear to my heart from my childhood, was the night my family and some close family friends took blankets outside on the lawn and star gazed. The kids were put out on blankets scattered along the yard and we just lay there watching the starry skies above. It was a clear night in our small town, and the sky was speckled with a trillion tiny, fiery lights that dotted the skies for as far as eye could see. From that night on, I have loved star gazing. Since the life span of a star can last billions of years, I like to think I may be looking at some of the same ones that I gazed at that long ago night as a child.

All those glorious stars that I gazed upon as a kid brings to mind our passage in Nehemiah. He alone made the heavens and all their starry host, everything on this earth and in the seas, everything! There is no other god but our Heavenly Father. He created those stars that shine high in the skies each night as well as all the other parts of creation we see, including us. How awe inspiring is this thought! As far as the eye can see do the stars in the sky go. It's breathtaking to look and marvel at all He has created.

This prayer in Nehemiah reminds us to praise the Lord for all His blessings and for the life He has breathed into us. Imagine as the Lord hears our prayers of praise, that He is looking down upon us. Wouldn't it be wonderful if our "praise prayers" were as numerous as those stars in the skies? Does He look down from heaven to see His people praying and praising Him? Just stop and imagine what that experience might be like. Can you envision being out in the country, no lights anywhere, and only the stars in the sky piece the darkness? Those stars go as far as our eyes can see each star representing each individual prayer. Our lives should be dedicated to serving Him, praising Him and praying to Him continuously. Yet we so easily get distracted.

Today, look to the skies and exalt His name, praying a prayer of awe and wonder over all He has made. He alone is worthy of our worship and praise. Let us shine like the stars in the night sky to all who see us, and may the Lord be pleased with our heartfelt prayers as we bow down before the Lord our God!

WEEK 6, DAY 3

Lord, we stand in awe of Your breath-taking creation. Only You could have created this amazing world we live in and the heavens above. Each piece of Your glorious world has a purpose. There is nothing and no one that could recreate such beauty. In Jesus' Name, amen.

Week 6, Day 4
Crazy, Beautiful You

For you created my inmost being; you knit me together in my mother's womb. I praise you because I am fearfully and wonderfully made; your works are wonderful, I know that full well.
Psalm 139:13

I love when I feel so deeply, I think my heart might burst. The depth of love, gratitude, awe and splendor fills me with warmth and excitement. The interesting thing is that there really isn't a word to accurately describe it. We have adjectives but nothing seems just perfect. Scientifically, our brains release chemicals that cause these feelings deep in our souls, but the actual feeling is simply hard to nail down. If we use words like "heart fluttering," "breathless," "astounding," "awe-inspiring," it still doesn't do justice to the depth of emotion. God has made this crazy, beautiful, unique being, complete with personality and life!

Our verse in Psalms clearly describes the wonder of God's incredible workmanship, the wonder of His creation of man. In Genesis 1:27 we know that He created man in "our image and after our likeness"; in Genesis 2:7 we know God formed us from "the dust of the ground," and we know from Genesis 2:21-22 that He formed woman "from the rib he had taken out of the man." Lastly, Luke 1:41 gives the account of Mary visiting Elizabeth and just her voice causes the baby in Elizabeth's womb to "leap." All of these verses show God's intricate workmanship from forming man from dust, and woman from the man's rib and, remarkably, He created us in His own image.

We have been intentionally created and knitted together while in the womb, meaning every fiber of our being has been hand-made by God Himself! The life moving inside the womb of Elizabeth with John the Baptist is just one example of how we interact with voices even *in utero*. We are extraordinary; we are intentional; we are a work of art made by God.

Only God understands the inner workings of the human organism and the attention to detail He put into each one of us that He created. What a work of complete art when we think of everything He put into each of our bodies both physically and spiritually! Deep within our souls we have emotions that can span from euphoric to dark and everything in between. Although I know in order to appreciate the highs, we must experience the lows, I love when I feel my soul leap for joy and when laughter bubbles up from within. Our amazing Father breathed life into our souls, and created an impossible-to-recreate, unique person found inside you! However, our emotions work, however indescribable our feelings, however unique our personal likes and loves, that wow factor inside of you is a gift from the Almighty! YOU are not a mistake! YOU were intentionally made to be none other than YOU!

Today, remember to thank God for all your happy moments, those sudden bursts of laughter, that comforting warmth of emotion that radiates through you as you go through your day. May your joyous nature be contagious to all around and may it bring Glory to God the Father! After all, He designed this crazy, beautiful You!

Lord God, we come before You and thank You for the miraculous craftmanship of the human body and soul. We thank You for creating us and for taking such intimate care as You created every fiber of our being. It is such a mystery that is still not completely understood. Thank You for this wonderful home for our soul on this earth. Help us to take care of it and to honor You. In Jesus' Name, amen.

Week 6, Day 5
Color Me Beautiful

*There he was transfigured before them.
His face shone like the sun, and his clothes
became as white as the light.*
Matthew 17:2

Did you know that white is technically not a color but a mixture of blue, red and green light? If you needed this color on a stage, those are the gel colors you would need to mix to make white. This shade is interesting because it is really the absence of color and it holds a lot of symbolism from ancient to modern times. In biblical times, white represented purity and forgiveness of sin. In modern times. a brand new bride wears a white dress to symbolize her purity and a baby being christened is dressed in white. But, although white symbolizes purity and innocence, it also has some negative connotations such as coldness or blandness. While white is the purest form of all colors, it does not get categorized as a color and instead it is more of a spectrum of color. It is truly amazing to see how it is used in many verses in the bible.

One such example of the descriptive use of white is found in Matthew 17, the transfiguration of Christ. Matthew speaks of how Jesus' face shone as the sun and His clothing became so white it looked like light. Can't you just imagine His clothing being so white, it was probably blinding? What an awesome vision for the witnesses, Peter, James, and John to behold! While watching this happen, they were also able to see Moses and Elijah. If this weren't enough, they heard God's voice from above say, "This is my Son, whom I love; with Him I am well pleased! Listen to Him!" At this moment God was speaking directly to Peter, James and John.

Imagine how these mere men felt seeing and hearing all of this take place. Once God's voice boomed from the heavens, the men fell face down in fear. Jesus being the friend He was, went to them, touched them and told them not to be afraid. He also asked them not to tell anyone what they saw. Oh how hard it would be not to tell everyone I saw about this occurrence! I would imagine at this point they were beginning to understand how much they did not understand about Jesus! What an amazing event to behold: their teacher and friend transformed right before their eyes! Did you notice that God used the purest form of color to clothe Jesus: absence of color equals absence of imperfection equals purity!

I do love white, and I love that it is used to describe such a miraculous transformation of Christ in the presence of God and men.

Today, be reminded every time you see anything white of Jesus' divine nature and glory. Relish the fact that we are His and look forward to the day we see Him coming in the clouds to gather His people!

WEEK 6, DAY 5

Lord, we cannot fathom what those disciples experienced during the transfiguration. I cannot imagine how overwhelming as well as indescribable that was to witness! Thank You for revealing Yourself to Jesus' disciples, and thank You for the scriptures that describe that event in time. We look forward to meeting Jesus in the sky and ultimately living in heaven with You. We give You all the glory, honor and praise ... in Jesus' Name, amen.

Week 6, Day 6
We're Free to Fly

Therefore, if anyone is in Christ, the new creation has come: The old has gone, the new is here!
2 Corinthians 5:17 NIV

A few years back I planted a lemon tree in a pot. I would go outside and sit beside it and inhale that heady scent of lemon from its creamy-colored flowers. One day I noticed this horrendous looking fat, bright green worm that had these red horns that would come out of its head. I looked him up and found his name was disgusting as well; he was a hornworm. I would mess with him just to see his red horns come out. It was mesmerizing to see something so ugly, yet so fascinating at the same time.

Then came the day I came out and he was gone and in his place was a chrysalis. Once my ugly friend finally emerged, I found myself looking at a hummingbird moth. Apparently, it is a rarity to see one of these moths and, honestly, I really found him quite beautiful. Although he didn't hang around long, I loved sitting outside in the sun,

WEEK 6, DAY 6

enjoying the peace of the afternoon with my ugly little worm friend. I missed him once he got his wings and flew off. I doubt he missed me though.

Yes, my hornworm was a new creation that came out with wings and was a much more handsome guy!!! This makes me think on this verse in 2 Corinthians 5: *"Therefore, if anyone is in Christ, the new creation has come: The old has gone, the new is here!"* God came to earth in human form as the Son of our Almighty God. Jesus lived a perfect human life on this earth, so He could die on a cross and pay the penalty for our sins. He broke down every barrier to the Father, so we could come before the throne blameless and pure. We are indeed a new creation! This is so like the transformation my hornworm experienced when he was given his wings.

I envision this ugly, green hornworm like me "before" Jesus. This poor worm had never experienced life outside of this lemon tree just as I had not experienced my freedom through Jesus. His food, his water and his very existence were all lived out on this small, potted lemon tree. Once he emerged from his chrysalis, he had wings to set him free just as Jesus set me free from sin and death. I am so grateful to be born again through Christ Jesus! I imagine how elated my hornworm was to find there was more to life than this one, small tree. He was free to live and experience life with his new wings.

We are free to fly!!! He broke the chains of sin and death!!! Don't anchor yourself to a tree like that worm but allow yourself the freedom to live out the blessed and abundant life that Christ paid for with His life! We don't have to be stuck living a life without wings, ugly and slow, chained to a limb of a tree. Say it aloud, "We are free to live a life in communion with the Father through His Son and the Holy Spirit. Thank You, Jesus." We no longer live a life of slavery to the old law condemned by our sinful nature. We are simply free to accept God's grace as we boldly confess Jesus as our one and only Savior.

Today, remember that your freedom comes from Christ's sacrifice. Enjoy the freedom, spread your wings and fly!

Lord God, we praise Your Holy Name! We are eternally grateful to You for sending Your Son to this earth to pay the ultimate price for our sins. I pray we step out in faith, and remember the life-changing sacrifice He suffered on the Cross. Just as the caterpillar transforms into a beautiful free-flying butterfly, so have You allowed us to also be transformed into the freedom only Christ can give. Thank You, Father! In Jesus' Name, amen.

Week 7
ATTRIBUTES AND ATTITUDES OF CHRIST IN US

How well do we really know our family, our friends or even Christ? How do we get to know and connect with someone? The answer is time. People are like onions with many layers. Over time, situations occur that reveal our heart to others and sometimes to ourselves.

Jesus has allowed us into His life through His Word and His Spirit. Just as we pick up little quirks from those around us, so do we also pick up little gems of inspiration from Christ. The more time we spend with Him, the more we emulate Him. This week, let's focus on how our attitudes convey our Love and life in Christ Jesus! May all His attributes be reflected in the way we live our lives every day!

Week 7, Day 1
Breathtaking Peace

He makes me lie down in green pastures,
he leads me beside quiet waters...
Psalm 23:2

When my son went to college in North Carolina, we took a family trip all the way from Texas to the Appalachian mountains to check out the state before he began his first semester. We found a nice vacation home rental in an area called Seven Devils, just a few hours' drive from his college. I loved it there. I can still envision the beauty and peace that surrounded that house there in the mountains of North Carolina. We had chipmunks that played around the house daily and trees and trails everywhere. I was at peace with nature and God! He created everything I saw out my window and I found a peace and contentment that I still feel in my soul as I think back on that idyllic place!

One morning, I decided to trek downhill a bit to see what was around. I found a trail through a thicket and as I emerged from the canopy, I came upon a large pond. The

WEEK 7, DAY 1

water was so clear, I could see all the fish swimming in it. I just stopped in amazement. I would never have seen this pond had I not walked this particular path through the trees. It was so tranquil and picturesque! The trees stood tall and mighty around the entire pond and the brilliant green grass that surrounded the water was perfectly mowed.

All I could hear was the stillness of the mountain, the chirping of the birds and the gentle wind that blew through my hair. Of course I had to stop and sit for a spell. I let the peace of God fill my soul and we had a little time together filled with breathtaking peace and serenity. I felt completely isolated from all the troubles of the world. This was my little sanctuary on the side of the mountain top in the foothills of North Carolina.

Psalm 23:2 says the Lord is my Shepherd, I shall lack nothing. He makes me lie down in green pastures. He leads me beside quiet waters. He restores my soul. David, the writer of this psalm, tried to obey God; he did find himself knee-deep in sin at times but David felt deep sorrow and he repented and turned back to God. Because of his great love for God, he is touted as a man after God's own heart in Acts 13:22. He was a man that felt deeply and loved heartily! His heart was human and devoted to the Almighty God. I like to envision him writing this prayer, feeling the way I felt as I sat by that tranquil pond in the mountains. Peace and comfort like no one or nothing could get to him. Just him and God, just me and God, just you and God.

Be still and pray this psalm and let His peace wash over you. David knew he could trust God and find refuge in Him. The same God that watched David now watches over us and gives us His peace in times of trouble. This is God! He is the same yesterday, today and tomorrow! He wants to grant us His peace.

Today, as we ruminate on Psalm 23, meditate on each verse, planting yourself in the descriptions given by David. Maybe you have a special place of serenity where you might reflect on these verses, a place where these words fit perfectly just like my pond in the foothills was a place where I could reflect on the Lord. Let the peace that surpasses all understanding fill your soul, and go through the day with a resolve to let God bless and guide your steps.

Father, You are our shepherd, You are our peace. You are our protector. Let us stop and be filled with the goodness and love that You bestow upon us. We love You and praise Your Holy Name! In Jesus' Name, amen.

Week 7, Day 2
Wisdom of the Spirit

*"No eye has seen, no ear has heard,
and no mind has imagined what God has prepared
for those who love him."*
1 Corinthians 2:9 NIV

The sky seems to go on forever and ever, it is so vast. The blues intermingle throughout the horizon and there is just no way to recreate its hue. How I love gazing into that azure sky! Scientists say all those different blues we see are due to the light waves scattering as they hit our atmosphere here on earth. As for me, I prefer to believe that it is just another one of God's indescribable miracles of beauty I get to appreciate every clear day.

Man craves to understand the world we live in as well as our own humanity. Scholars and scientists write books of modern knowledge that in turn get taught to us from an early age. They do this in the hope of enlightening us according to their understanding of the world around us. We have libraries full of tomes that cover every topic under the sun including our enchanting blue sky. Are we ready to learn? But none of the knowledge we have at our fingertips can ever truly unravel the mysteries of God's incredible creation.

God knows we are curious by nature, and He wants to unveil His wisdom to us through the study of His Word and the guidance of His Spirit. In 1 Corinthians 2:3 Paul wrote of the wisdom of the Spirit of God and the power of the Spirit. He says that our faith should not rest on men's wisdom but on God's power. It's the same power that spoke that blue sky into existence: our God, creator of the heavens and the earth, man and spirit, animal and insect, the seen and the unseen.

God speaks a spiritual language that cannot be understood by man without the Spirit inside of him to open his eyes. With only his human understanding, man will never even come close to understanding what God has unveiled for us. As we pore over His Word, our eyes, ears and minds are opened to His Truth. With God, the more we seek, the more we find!

Let's become scholars of His Word. When all of this passes away, it will not matter if we understand what made the skies blue; but it will matter if we lived a Spirit-led life.

Today, as you look to that clear blue sky, let it be a reminder to keep studying the Word, and to keep our mind fully present and engaged, so the Spirit that lives within us can speak to us the secret wisdom of God. Let us get our PHD in His Holy Word.

Lord God, as we come to You today, open our eyes and our hearts, so You can unveil Yourself to us. May the Holy Spirit guide us as we study the scriptures. We are so thankful for You, Lord, God, Jesus, and the Holy Spirit. In Jesus' Name, amen.

Week 7, Day 3
Rockin' It

For in scripture, it says: "See, I lay a stone in Zion, a chosen and precious cornerstone, and the one who trusts in him will never be put to shame."
1 Peter 2:6

Whenever I travel, I like to pick up a rock or stone as a souvenir. I place them in my garden and I can remember where I picked up each one. This is because I choose my stones with distinctive attributes that can help me distinguish one from the other. My son has a tumbled stone he asked me to buy for him in San Antonio. It's amazing how perfect these stones are ... they tumble against one another and come out so shiny and smooth. How in the world can something so dirty and imperfect knock about and turn into something so well-formed? It just baffles my mind that there are no sharp edges anywhere on them. They have become perfect rocks!

Perfect. When it comes to that word the only thing that ever comes to mind is Jesus, the only perfect human being to ever walk this earth—Jesus, who remained sinless yet allowed Himself to be hung on a cross as the ultimate sacrifice for our sins. 1 Peter 2: 4-12 is all about the living stone. It speaks of the stone that is laid in Zion, the city of David, the new Jerusalem that is written of in Revelation. Jesus is both the capstone and the Living Stone.

As followers of Jesus, we are constantly being honed by the Spirit, to be more like Jesus every day. As we stumble and tumble through our lives, and strive to be perfected in Him, we too can come out each time smoother and shinier than ever. Will we ever come out perfect? No. But through His mercy and love, we can continually be working towards that marvelous eternal perfection we will find in heaven.

Some people give the illusion that they have already found their perfection. Their lives look so whole and all together; but we know that is an illusion. No one here on earth has that luxury, nor would we want to be viewed as perfect. Without life's bumps and bruises, we wouldn't have the opportunity to stretch and grow our spiritual selves. We would never be able to have empathy for others. Instead of complaining, "Why me?" let's say, "Why not me?" Lord, show me what I need to learn. Look and see how we have grown through the storms, and thank the Lord for the ability to see His glory through them.

Let those tumbled stones be a reminder that, through our obedience and devotion to Christ, we get to come out of this world like those smooth and perfect stones. In heaven, we will be our best selves, our perfect selves through Jesus. Can I hear an amen? How wonderful that day will be!!!

Today, let us view our trials through the lens of that smooth and perfect stone. Pick up a rock today and view all its rough edges and the dirt that mars it. Imagine it all

WEEK 7, DAY 3

smooth and clean. Let it be a reminder that we are continuously being refined so that we can one day glorify our Lord in heaven.

Lord God, we come before You as imperfect and sinful people. However, by Your grace and mercy, You sent Jesus as the perfector of our faith. Through Jesus we can be transformed into the smooth and flawless stone tumbled to perfection through the blood of Christ. Thank You Father! Through His love and mercy, we pray, amen.

Week 7, Day 4
Sweet Memories

Offer hospitality to one another without grumbling.
1 Peter 4:9

When I was growing up, there was this precious couple, Mr. and Mrs. Robbins who lived down the street as well as attended my church. They were such wonderful people and were always happy to see me and whatever friend I might have in tow come over for a visit. Mrs. Robbins was an artist that was always happy to show me what she was painting, and Mr. Robbins was a gardener that loved to show off what he had blooming out back. I remember his gardens felt like a maze and each section he had would be completely different. When I was older, I recalled him wanting to play dominoes and the story he told me of his delight over opening a new bar of soap. Meanwhile, Mrs. Robbins would bring in some fresh-baked cookies and lemonade.

    The contented happiness of that family has stayed in my heart all these years, and I cherish the memories of my

WEEK 7, DAY 4

visits with them. When I think of hospitality, I am always reminded of the Robbins.

This couple demonstrated I Peter 4:9 perfectly. They always had their doors open to people and their hearts were as open as their doors. They never complained. They were as beloved on our street as they were in our congregation. As easy as they made it look, I know from experience it wasn't always that easy. We get absorbed in our lives and it gets hard to squeeze in time for guests, both expected and unexpected.

I want to practice the art of hospitality done the Robbins way. No matter what I have going on, I want to be able to stop and enjoy my time with whomever has blessed me with a visit. I would like to be part of some sweet memories with those that drop into my life. I don't want to be worried about how my home looks or worried about how much I need to get done. I just want to be an open door of warmth and love.

Being hospitable is important to God. He wants us to be part of the fabric of others' lives. It's been over forty years since I've seen the Robbins but every time I open a bar of soap, I think of Mr. Robbins. It wasn't the story that left an imprint on my mind, but the time spent with a kid that had nothing to offer him and his wife but innocence. Can you imagine being that memory for someone long after you are gone? What we do today can be that "moment" in someone's life that lasts long after we have passed on to the afterlife. Just a listening ear, a cup of coffee or a sit on the porch ... just a willingness to give someone a bit of your time and attention is so meaningful.

Today, thank God for those who have helped shape your

SWEET MEMORIES

life by their hospitality and the sweet memories they have given you. Just as a bar of soap reminds me of how I should be 1 Peter 4:9 to others, let whatever jiggles your memory serve as your reminder as well. Who knows, long after you're gone, you may be a sweet memory to someone, and you never even knew it! Let's honor God with our hospitality at every opportunity we have!

Lord God, we thank You for the people You have put upon our paths. We are so thankful for those who have been hospitable to us. Lord, please open our hearts to being more humble and more loving. We pray for opportunities to be that open door to others. Let us radiate Your warmth and love everywhere and always. Thank You, Almighty God, for Your continuous blessings upon us! In Jesus' Name, amen.

Week 7, Day 5
The Gift of Friendship

Oil and perfume make the heart glad, and the sweetness of a friend comes from his earnest counsel.
Proverbs 27:9 NIV

Have you ever had a friend you can be yourself with? They are everything you are not and vice versa. In all our wonderful, quirky ways we have found someone to do life with. I read one time that some researchers discovered that as early as six months, friendships were observed in babies. To me, that is incredible. From birth, we are drawn to certain people God has put into our paths. To sweeten the deal, these wonderful gifts from the Lord give us another person to receive godly counsel from in our journey in this life.

Good, godly friendships are nothing short of a God-blessed miracle. When we find ourselves with friends that our souls just mesh with, and we feel as if we were part of a puzzle. All the pieces fit perfectly. That is just God! I know that I have good and bad days, and that only someone brought to me by God could put up with all my "me moments."

THE GIFT OF FRIENDSHIP

When we join our lives with another Christian, isn't it so nice to have someone we can talk to about our good times and bad, our ideas and our dreams, our faith, our joys, our trials and our fears. Sharing life with someone you can truly be yourself with and talk about anything and everything is a gift from God. The love I feel for my close friends fills my heart with joy and thankfulness.

Let's look at Proverbs 27:9. We all need trustworthy and godly friends. How much more do we need someone from whom we can receive godly advice! How do we know if their counsel is in alignment with God? Any advice that is based in prayer and knowledge of the Truth found in the Bible is a great place to start. Sometimes, we just need someone to help us unravel a problem or work through a situation. How great is our Father to provide us not only friendships but those that have a foundation in Christ! Wow! This is the joy that we are reading of in this passage.

One aspect of godly friendship is that there is always room for more. I fully believe we have older friendships that have been cultivated over a long period of time. Those are such a lovely gift from God but always keep the door open as we never know when God has someone new to drop into our lives. Sometimes those people fit perfectly into our other relationships and sometimes they are just yours to treasure. No matter new or old, it is important to realize that God has gifted us with these relationships, and He has united us to walk our Christian path together.

Today, let's make it a point to reach out to a friend and tell them what a blessing they are to you! Let them know that your friendship is a gift from God above!

WEEK 7, DAY 5

Lord, we thank You for the brothers and sisters in Christ You have blessed us with and how they weave right into the tapestry of our lives. We thank You that we can worship together, play together, and encourage each other. Lord, open our eyes to new friendships You bring along. May we cultivate them into a deep and loving friendship. Thank You for friends both new and old ... they are all indeed a blessing from You. In Jesus' Name, amen.

Week 7, Day 6
Strength Training 101

> *Moses was a hundred and twenty years old*
> *when he died, yet his eyes were not weak,*
> *nor his strength gone.*
> Deuteronomy 34:7

You just can't turn on the television without seeing an ad for some gadget or pill that will help strengthen your body and allow you to live a longer, stronger, healthier life. All it takes is a devotion to exercise or diet or this pill or whatever. You'd think we would all be looking to live as long as Methuselah. Um . . . over 900 years? No thanks. Moses though, lived to be 120 and that sounds okay, especially when we find out he didn't suffer the effects of aging! He didn't rely on any pills or exercise regimes for his body that just wouldn't quit. He relied on a very big and powerful God. Through a life of devotion and submission to God, he was blessed with a body that could carry him through his forty-year trek through the wilderness.

Our verse in Deuteronomy 34:7 is a great teaching

WEEK 7, DAY 6

moment for us today. Although Moses was one of the blessed ones that lived to a ripe old age in perfect health, he didn't live a life of ease. After all, he was charged with freeing God's people from a very powerful ruler, was thus chased through a body of water, then wandered over miles and miles of desert with a bunch of grumbling people! Throughout this entire scenario he was privy to a number of interactions with God. Imagine talking with God and performing miracles that God did through you? Wow! Moses was blessed because of a life of submission and devotion to the Lord. In turn, the Lord blessed him with a good strong body and mind. Move over Peloton, out of the way, vitamin man, we have something better! Moses had God!!!!

Moses had a goal, given by God to get His people to the Promised Land. For forty years he took care of many thousands of people along the way who were prone to complaining. How easy it would have been to get disheartened! This wasn't Moses though. He had a determination to stay true to God, follow Him both day and night and to get the package to the destination safely. Sadly, humanity overtook him and he disobeyed God during a weak moment involving a staff and a rock in Numbers 20:7-12. The Israelites were grumbling about thirst, AGAIN, and God told Moses to speak to the rock; instead he struck it twice. Sadly, this moment of weakness of misrepresenting God to the people is what cost Moses his ticket into the Promised Land.

I cannot imagine how frustrated Moses must have felt. But one thing Moses did not do was rebel in anger against God. Because of the great love Moses had for God and his life of submission to Him, he was blessed with this incredible stamina! Yes, he grew old but that old timer still had

STRENGTH TRAINING 101

perfect eyesight and great strength. His devotion and love to God was what his life was all about!

Blessings are found in our lives, and we don't want to miss them because we are off grumbling about something or give in to world weariness. We were made for more than we can ever imagine! Can I hear an amen! No vitamin or gym can provide such wonderful results as a life lived in obedience to God.

Today, think back on all the lessons we can glean from Moses. As we move through our day, watch for ways to be submissive to God. One day when we are at the end of our journey, we can enjoy all the blessings He has given us for living a life of devotion to Him. I think I'll skip the gym today and hit the bible for a little exercise!

Lord God, thank You for the example we have in the life of Moses. Let him be an encouragement as to how to live our lives as a living sacrifice to You. May we stop and take time to notice the blessings You have heaped upon us. Help us not to tire or grow weary but to stay focused on You until the day You call us home. In Jesus' Name, amen.

I hope you have enjoyed these seven weeks of devotionals. There is nothing more grounding to me and my faith than being hyper aware of the Lord in my own personal world. In writing this book, I spent many hours outside in His Presence. I just let Him lead my eyes and mind to whatever He had in store for me that day. Even as I go back through these devotionals, I find a sweet time of intimacy with Him that I cherish. Somehow, He always has something new to teach me!

God reveals Himself through His glorious creation every day, and I love doing life with Him. I can only hope this has inspired you to find Him in your world as well. He leaves gentle reminders of His incredible love, faithfulness and mercy everywhere and every day. It's been a privilege to stop with each one of you, and take notice of our wonderful, awe-inspiring God.

www.ingramcontent.com/pod-product-compliance
Lightning Source LLC
Chambersburg PA
CBHW070545090426
42735CB00013B/3072